GoodFood

101 BEST-EVER  RECIPES

10 9 8 7

Published in 2008 by BBC Books,
an imprint of Ebury Publishing
A Random House Group Company

Photographs © BBC Magazines 2008
Recipes © BBC Magazines 2008
Book design © Woodlands Books Ltd 2008
All the recipes contained in this book first
appeared in BBC *Good Food* magazine.

The Random House Group Limited
Reg. No. 954009

Addresses for companies within the
Random House Group can be found at
www.randomhouse.co.uk

A CIP catalogue record for this book is
available from the British Library.

The Random House Group Limited supports
The Forest Stewardship Council (FSC), the
leading international forest certification organization.
All our titles that are printed on Greenpeace
approved FSC certified paper carry the FSC logo.
Our paper procurement policy can be found at
www.rbooks.co.uk/environment

To buy books by your favourite authors and
register for offers visit www.rbooks.co.uk

Printed and bound by Firmengruppe APPL,
aprinta druck, Wemding, Germany
Colour origination by Dot Gradations Ltd, UK

Commissioning Editor: Lorna Russell
Project Editor: Laura Higginson
Designer: Annette Peppis
Jacket Design: Kathryn Gammon
Production: David Brimble
Picture Researchers: Gabby Harrington
and Natalie Lief

ISBN: 9781846074349

GoodFood

101 BEST-EVER CHICKEN RECIPES
TRIED-AND-TESTED IDEAS

Editor
Jeni Wright

BOOKS

Contents

Introduction

Where would we be without chicken? Quick and easy to cook, tender and low fat, it's the ideal ingredient for everyday meals and special occasions. It's the perfect solution for tricky dinner guests, too: even those who don't like red meat will almost always eat chicken.

In this collection of 101 recipes we've chosen the best chicken dishes ever published in *Good Food Magazine* and brought them together so you can quickly and easily find your favourites, no matter who you're cooking for or what the occasion. And with every recipe tried and tested in the *Good Food* kitchen, you can't possibly go wrong.

In this book you'll be spoilt for choice for what to cook: whether it's a family supper for you and the kids, a Friday-night curry for friends, or an impressive dinner-party dish to pull out all the stops. There are even light and healthy dishes if you're watching your weight ... and dishes that can be on the table in less than 20 minutes if you're watching the clock.

If all this isn't enough, there's also a chapter of classic recipes from around the world – to evoke happy memories of holiday meals and inspire you to re-create them at home.

Jeni Wright
BBC Good Food Magazine

Notes and Conversion tables

NOTES ON THE RECIPES
• Eggs are large in the UK and Australia unless stated otherwise.
• Wash all fresh produce before preparation.
• Recipes contain nutritional analyses for 'sugar', which means the total sugar content including all natural sugars in the ingredients unless otherwise stated.

OVEN TEMPERATURES

Gas	°C	Fan °C	°F	Oven temp.
¼	110	90	225	Very cool
½	120	100	250	Very cool
1	140	120	275	Cool or slow
2	150	130	300	Cool or slow
3	160	140	325	Warm
4	180	160	350	Moderate
5	190	170	375	Moderately hot
6	200	180	400	Fairly hot
7	220	200	425	Hot
8	230	210	450	Very hot
9	240	220	475	Very hot

APPROXIMATE WEIGHT CONVERSIONS
• All the recipes in this book list both imperial and metric measurements. Conversions are approximate and have been rounded up or down. Follow one set of measurements only; do not mix the two.
• Cup measurements, which are used by cooks in Australia and America, have not been listed here as they vary from ingredient to ingredient. Kitchen scales should be used to measure dry/solid ingredients.

SPOON MEASURES

Spoon measurements are level unless otherwise specified.

- 1 teaspoon (tsp) = 5ml
- 1 tablespoon (tbsp) = 15ml
- 1 Australian tablespoon = 20ml (cooks in Australia should measure 3 teaspoons where 1 tablespoon is specified in a recipe)

APPROXIMATE LIQUID CONVERSIONS

metric	imperial	AUS	US
50ml	2fl oz	¼ cup	¼ cup
125ml	4fl oz	½ cup	½ cup
175ml	6fl oz	¾ cup	¾ cup
225ml	8fl oz	1 cup	1 cup
300ml	10fl oz/½ pint	½ pint	1¼ cups
450ml	16fl oz	2 cups	2 cups/1 pint
600ml	20fl oz/1 pint	1 pint	2½ cups
1 litre	35fl oz/1¾ pints	1¾ pints	1 quart

This dish is already low in fat, but to make it even lighter omit the chorizo and add two teaspoons of smoked paprika to the softened onion, then remove the chicken skin before serving.

Chicken and Rice One-pot

4 chicken breasts, skin on
50g/2oz chorizo sausage, skinned and cut into chunks (or slices from a pack)
1 large onion, roughly chopped
200g/8oz basmati rice
500ml/18fl oz hot chicken stock
400g can red kidney beans in water, drained and rinsed
few fresh thyme sprigs or ½ tsp dried thyme
handful of pitted green olives

Takes 30 minutes • Serves 4 (easily halved)

1 Heat a flameproof casserole and dry fry the chicken, skin-side down, for 8 minutes until golden, turning halfway through. Pour off any excess fat. Tip in the chorizo and fry for a minute until it releases its oil. Remove the chicken and chorizo and fry the onion in the remaining oil for 3 minutes, until softened.
2 Tip in the rice, stir to mix with the onion then return the chicken and chorizo to the pan. Pour in the stock, add the remaining ingredients and season to taste. Cover and cook over a medium heat for 10 minutes, or until the chicken is cooked through and the rice is fluffy.

• Per serving 462 kcalories, protein 43g, carbohydrate 57g, fat 8g, saturated fat 3g, fibre 5g, added sugar none, salt 2.28g

This is delicious cooked under the grill or on the barbecue and served with new potatoes and a green salad.

Lemon and Five-spice Chicken

2 lemons
3 tbsp light muscovado sugar
thumb-sized piece fresh root
ginger, shredded (no need to peel)
2 garlic cloves, peeled and crushed
5 tbsp soy sauce
½ tsp Chinese five-spice powder
splash of dry sherry or dry
white wine
8 chicken thighs on the bone,
skin on

Takes 25 minutes, plus marinating •
Serves 4 (easily doubled)

1 Juice one lemon and cut the other into slices, then put both into a large plastic food bag with all the other ingredients and shake well to coat the chicken. Leave for at least 10 minutes, or up to 24 hours in the fridge.
2 Heat the grill to high or fire up the barbecue. Remove the chicken from the marinade, shake off the excess, then grill or barbecue for 20 minutes until golden brown and cooked through. During cooking, turn the chicken over occasionally and baste with the marinade.

• Per serving 493 kcalories, protein 50g, carbohydrate 7g, fat 30g, saturated fat 9g, fibre none, sugar 7g, salt 2.25g

This dish is really healthy: high in fibre, a good source of iron, folic acid and vitamin C, and the veg count as two of your five-a-day.

Frying-pan Chicken

1 tbsp olive oil
2 skinless chicken thighs
200g/8oz potatoes, cut into chunks
2 carrots, thickly sliced
1 parsnip, thickly sliced
2 tsp wholegrain mustard
1 small glass dry white wine or chicken stock

Takes 40–45 minutes • Serves 1

1 Heat the oil in a large frying pan (which has a lid), add the chicken and fry until golden. Turn over and fry for a further 2 minutes. Remove from the pan, add the vegetables and fry over a fairly high heat until they start to colour.

2 Return the chicken to the pan and season with salt and pepper. Add the mustard and wine or stock and bring to the boil. Reduce the heat, cover the pan and simmer gently for 25–30 minutes, or until the chicken is cooked through and the vegetables are tender. Add a splash of water if the sauce starts to become dry.

• Per serving 734 kcalories, protein 59g, carbohydrate 72g, fat 21g, saturated fat 4g, fibre 14g, sugar 28g, salt 1.41g

As well as being low in fat, this dish is also a good source of vitamin C and the tomatoes count as one of your five-a-day fruit and veg.

Tagliatelle with Grilled Chicken

500g/1lb 2oz boneless skinless
chicken breasts
finely grated zest and juice of
1 lemon
1 tbsp chopped fresh tarragon leaves
or 1 tsp dried
2 tsp olive oil
8 small tomatoes, halved
300g/10oz tagliatelle

Takes 20–25 minutes • Serves 4

1 Heat grill to high. Coat the chicken with the lemon zest and juice, tarragon and salt and pepper. Put in a shallow, flameproof dish or roasting tin in one layer. Brush with a little oil then grill for 6 minutes. Turn the chicken over and add the tomatoes, cut-side up, then brush with oil. Grill for a further 6–8 minutes until the chicken is cooked through and lightly browned and the tomatoes are tender.
2 Meanwhile, cook the pasta in a large pan of salted boiling water according to the packet instructions. Drain well, reserving 150ml/¼ pint of the cooking water, then return to the pan.
3 Remove the chicken from the dish and cut into bite-size chunks. Toss into the pasta with the juices from the dish, the tomatoes and the measured cooking water.

• Per serving 423 kcalories, protein 40g, carbohydrate 61g, fat 4g, saturated fat 1g, fibre 3g, sugar 4g, salt 0.48g

To spice this up a little, use cooked, tandoori-spiced chicken breasts and use chopped coriander or mint in the yoghurt dressing instead of tarragon.

Roast Chicken and Potato Salad

500g bag new potatoes, halved if large
1 ready-roasted chicken (about 900g/2lb), or ready-roasted chicken breasts for speed
150g carton low-fat natural yoghurt
1 tbsp clear honey
handful of fresh tarragon leaves, roughly chopped
225g bag salad leaves
4 roasted red peppers from a jar, sliced

Takes 25 minutes • Serves 4

1 Boil or steam the potatoes for 15–20 minutes until tender, then cool quickly in cold water (it's fine if they're still slightly warm) and drain. Pull the meat off the roast chicken, or take the chicken breasts and tear into bite-sized pieces.

2 Make the dressing by mixing the yoghurt with the honey and tarragon and season to taste. Toss the salad leaves, peppers, chicken and potatoes in a large bowl, drizzle the dressing over, then serve immediately.

• Per serving 440 kcalories, protein 37g, carbohydrate 32g, fat 19g, saturated fat 4g, fibre 3g, sugar 3g, salt 1.48g

A speedy dish from just four ingredients – all this needs to accompany it are green beans and sautéed or roast potatoes. If you prefer, spread the chicken with tomato relish or salsa instead.

Tangy Chicken Breasts

2 boneless skinless chicken breasts
3 tbsp barbecue sauce
2 rashers streaky bacon
50g/2oz Cheddar, grated

Takes 25 minutes • Serves 2
(easily doubled)

1 Heat the grill to medium-high and line a baking sheet with foil. Lay the chicken upside-down on the foil, brush with one tablespoon of the barbecue sauce, and grill for 5 minutes. Turn the chicken breasts over and add the bacon rashers to the tray. Grill for a further 5 minutes.

2 Drizzle the chicken with the remaining barbecue sauce and sprinkle with the cheese. Grill for 2–3 minutes until the chicken is cooked through, the cheese is bubbling and golden and the bacon is crisp.

• Per serving 321 kcalories, protein 42g, carbohydrate 6g, fat 14g, saturated fat 8g, fibre none, sugar 6g, salt 2.38g

A really satisfying sandwich that's surprisingly low in fat.

Chicken Caesar Sandwich

2 boneless skinless chicken breasts
1 tsp sunflower oil
2 Little Gem lettuces
2 tbsp low-fat crème fraîche or thick Greek yoghurt
1 tbsp grated Parmesan, plus a few shavings to serve
squeeze of fresh lemon juice
1 tsp capers, roughly chopped
2 thick slices of bread
1 small garlic clove, peeled and cut in half

Takes 20 minutes • Serves 2

1 Heat a griddle pan. Rub the chicken with the oil, season with salt and pepper, then griddle for 7 minutes on each side or until cooked through. Set aside to rest.
2 Meanwhile, separate the lettuce leaves. Mix the crème fraîche, Parmesan, lemon juice and capers with one tablespoon cold water, then season to taste.
3 Toast the bread and rub with the cut side of the garlic, then crush the garlic and add it to the dressing. Slice the warm chicken breasts on the diagonal, then top the toast with lettuce leaves, sliced chicken breast and a drizzle of the Caesar dressing. Finish with a few shavings of Parmesan.

• Per sandwich 319 kcalories, protein 40g, carbohydrate 24g, fat 8g, saturated fat 3g, fibre 2g, sugar 3g, salt 1.01g

A super-simple hotpot to warm you up on a cold day.

Chicken, Squash and Potato Hotpot

¼ small butternut squash, peeled and diced (about 200g/8oz)

8 small new potatoes

1 tsp ground coriander

few fresh thyme sprigs

600ml/1 pint chicken stock

1 garlic clove, peeled and crushed

2 boneless skinless chicken breasts

25g/1oz pitted green olives in brine, drained

175g/6oz prepared French beans, courgettes or broccoli

Takes 45 minutes • Serves 2 (easily doubled)

1 Pre-heat the oven to 190°C/Gas 5/fan 170°C. Put the squash, potatoes, coriander, thyme, stock and garlic into a flameproof casserole. Season and bring to the boil, then simmer gently for 10 minutes.

2 Tuck in the chicken breasts, making sure they are submerged. Cover and transfer to the oven for 15 minutes, or until the chicken is cooked through. Lift out the chicken and vegetables and keep warm, then boil the stock until reduced by half. Add the olives and green vegetables and simmer until they are cooked, then season and serve with the chicken.

• Per serving 413 kcalories, protein 41g, carbohydrate 50g, fat 6.5g, saturated fat 1.5g, fibre 8g, sugar 13g, salt 1g

This easy one-pot dish is perfect for an informal dinner party – it cooks by itself in the oven while you entertain your guests.

Chicken with Roots and Chickpeas

4 chicken legs, skin on
4 carrots, cut into large chunks
3 parsnips, cut into large chunks
1 onion, peeled and cut into large chunks
2 tbsp olive oil
1 tbsp Moroccan seasoning
400g can chickpeas, drained and rinsed
400g can chopped tomatoes
handful of fresh coriander leaves, chopped

Takes approx. 1 hour • Serves 4

1 Pre-heat the oven to 220°C/Gas 7/fan 200°C. Put the chicken and the vegetables in a roasting tin and toss in the oil and seasoning. Roast for 40 minutes, shaking the tin occasionally.

2 When the chicken and vegetables are cooked, lift the chicken on to plates and put the roasting tin over a high heat on the hob. Tip in the chickpeas and tomatoes and bring to a simmer. Cook for a few minutes then stir in the coriander. Serve with the chicken.

• Per serving 590 kcalories, protein 40g, carbohydrate 37g, fat 32g, saturated fat 8g, fibre 10g, sugar 17g, salt 2.1g

Although creamy in both name and texture, this soup contains no cream. Packed with generous chunks of chicken and vegetables, it's a complete meal in a bowl.

Creamy Chicken Soup

85g/3oz butter
1 small onion, peeled and roughly chopped
1 large carrot, cut into small chunks
2 small King Edward or red-skinned potatoes (about 300g/10oz), cut into small chunks (no need to peel)
1 large leek, trimmed and thinly sliced
1 heaped tbsp fresh thyme leaves, plus extra to serve
50g/2oz plain flour
1.3 litres/2¼ pints hot chicken stock
200–250g/8–9oz boneless skinless cooked chicken, torn into large chunks
grated fresh nutmeg, to taste

Takes 40 minutes • Serves 4

1 Heat one-third of the butter in a large, wide pan until bubbling, and fry the onion for 3–4 minutes until just starting to colour. Stir in the carrot and potatoes and fry for 4 minutes, then add the leek and thyme and cook for 3 minutes more. Set aside.
2 Heat the remaining butter in a medium saucepan (preferably non-stick) until bubbling. Stir in the flour and keep stirring for 3–4 minutes until pale golden. Pour in the hot stock gradually, beating well after each addition, then stir into the vegetables and bring to a simmer. Cook very gently for 8–10 minutes, stirring occasionally.
3 Stir in the chicken, nutmeg and seasoning to taste. Warm through, and serve piping hot with a grinding of pepper and a scattering of thyme leaves.

• Per serving 449 kcalories, protein 28g, carbohydrate 32g, fat 24g, saturated fat 13g, fibre 4g, sugar 8g, salt 1.10g

Give the vegetables lots of room in the tin when roasting – overcrowding will slow down the cooking and cause them to steam rather than roast.

Roasted Ratatouille Chicken

1 onion, cut into wedges
2 red peppers, peeled and seeded and cut into chunks
1 courgette, cut into chunks
1 small aubergine, cut into chunks
4 tomatoes, halved
4 tbsp olive oil, plus extra for drizzling
4 chicken breasts, skin on
few fresh rosemary sprigs (optional)

Takes 50 minutes • Serves 4 (easily halved)

1 Pre-heat the oven to 200°C/Gas 6/fan 180°C. Lay all the vegetables in a roasting tin, spreading them out evenly. Pour in the olive oil and mix until everything is well coated (hands are easiest for this).
2 Put the chicken breasts, skin-side up, on top of the vegetables and tuck in some rosemary sprigs, if using. Season with salt and black pepper and drizzle a little oil over the chicken. Roast for about 35 minutes until the vegetables are soft and the chicken is golden and cooked through. Drizzle with oil before serving.

• Per serving 318 kcalories, protein 37g, carbohydrate 13g, fat 14g, saturated fat 2g, fibre 4g, added sugar none, salt 0.25g

The ultimate in comfort food, these wraps look smart with very little effort – there's no rolling, no trimming and no waste.

No-roll Chicken Wraps

4 tbsp olive oil
200g pack chestnut mushrooms, sliced
handful of fresh parsley leaves, chopped
1 plump garlic clove, peeled and crushed
375g pack ready-rolled puff pastry (rectangular, not round)
4 boneless skinless chicken breasts
1 egg, beaten
green vegetable or salad, to serve (optional)

Takes 40–50 minutes • Serves 4

1 Pre-heat the oven to 220°C/Gas 7/fan 200°C with a baking sheet inside. Heat two tablespoons of the oil in a frying pan, add the mushrooms and fry over a high heat for 3 minutes until golden and just cooked. Toss in the parsley and garlic, season generously and set aside to cool slightly.
2 Unroll the pastry and cut into quarters. Sit a chicken breast diagonally in the middle of each piece of pastry. Spoon the mushroom mixture over the chicken and drizzle over the remaining oil. Bring two opposite corners of the pastry together over the chicken and mushrooms so they just overlap, then pinch together. Brush the pastry with the egg. Carefully transfer the parcels to the hot baking sheet using a fish slice and bake for 30 minutes until puffed up and golden.

• Per serving 624 kcalories, protein 42g, carbohydrate 35g, fat 36g, saturated fat 12g, fibre 1g, added sugar none, salt 1g

This bright, colourful dish is packed with folic acid – a B vitamin that helps our bodies break down and use proteins, and keeps our blood healthy.

Broccoli, Chicken and Cashew Stir Fry

1 tbsp soy sauce
2 tsp seasoned rice vinegar or white wine vinegar
juice of 1 small orange
1 tsp dark muscovado sugar
2 tsp cornflour
2 tbsp stir-fry oil or vegetable oil
85g/3oz unsalted cashew nuts
1 onion, peeled and thinly sliced
1 large boneless skinless chicken breast, cut into chunks
250g/9oz broccoli florets
150g pack mangetout, sliced in half
1 red pepper, seeded and thinly sliced

Takes 20–30 minutes • Serves 2

1 In a jug, mix together the soy sauce, vinegar, orange juice, sugar and cornflour.
2 Heat the oil in a wok. Add the cashews and cook for a minute until golden brown. Remove the nuts and tip on to kitchen paper to drain. Add the onion and fry over a high heat for 3–5 minutes until browned and softened, then lift out and add to the cashews.
3 Tip the chicken into the wok and stir fry for 3–4 minutes. Add the broccoli, mangetout and red pepper. Stir fry for 4–5 minutes, or until the chicken is cooked through and the vegetables are tender, yet still crunchy.
4 Stir the cornflour mixture to blend the ingredients, pour into the wok and stir fry for a couple of minutes until the sauce thickens. Stir in the cooked onion and cashews then pile on to warm plates.

• Per serving 583 kcalories, protein 37g, carbohydrate 34g, fat 34g, saturated fat 4g, fibre 9g, sugar 3g, salt 1.83g

The only other ingredients you'll need with this heavenly dish are some new potatoes and a green salad on the side.

Sticky Lemon Chicken

4 part-boned chicken breasts, skin on
finely grated zest and juice of 1 large lemon
1 tbsp clear honey
1 tbsp olive oil
2 garlic cloves, peeled and chopped
1 tsp dried oregano

Takes 45 minutes • Serves 4

1 Pre-heat the oven to 190°C/Gas 5/fan 170°C. Put the chicken breasts, skin-side up, in a roasting tin. Put all the remaining ingredients in a bowl and warm through in the microwave or in a small pan for 1 minute, then stir to mix everything together and pour over the chicken.

2 Transfer the tin to the oven and roast the chicken for 30 minutes or until cooked through, basting every 10 minutes or so. The juices will gradually thicken and give the chicken a shiny coating at the end. Leave to stand for 5 minutes before serving.

• Per serving 250 kcalories, protein 31g, carbohydrate 4g, fat 13g, saturated fat 3g, fibre none, sugar 3g, salt 0.23g

Spice up your life with this low-fat, no-cook recipe. It can also be made with leftover cooked rice.

Spicy Chicken Rice

250g pouch pre-cooked rice
200g pack spicy or sweet chilli cooked chicken fillets
⅓ cucumber, finely chopped
2 carrots, coarsely grated
20g pack fresh mint, leaves chopped
150g carton low-fat natural yoghurt
1 tsp clear honey
pinch of chilli powder

Takes 15 minutes • Serves 2

1 Cook the rice according to packet instructions. Chop the chicken into bite-sized pieces. Mix the rice and chicken with the cucumber and carrots in a large bowl.
2 Mix half the mint with the yoghurt, honey, chilli powder and seasoning. Stir into the rice mixture and sprinkle with the remaining mint.

• Per serving 357 kcalories, protein 31g, carbohydrate 57g, fat 2g, saturated fat 1g, fibre 3g, sugar 19g, salt 0.99g

With an all-in-one sauce that you can prepare ahead, this is an ideal weeknight supper for the family. Serve with a crisp green salad.

Chicken and Pesto Roll-ups

25g/1oz butter
25g/1oz plain flour
600ml/1 pint milk
100g/4oz Gruyère, grated
50g/2oz Parmesan, grated
6 tbsp pesto, from a jar
8 ready-made pancakes
2 boneless skinless cooked chicken breasts, shredded
285g jar artichoke hearts in oil, drained and quartered if necessary

Takes 50 minutes–1 hour • Serves 4

1 Pre-heat the oven to 200°C/Gas 6/fan 180°C. Put the butter, flour and milk in a pan. Whisk over a medium heat until mixture boils and thickens. Reduce the heat and simmer for 5 minutes. Remove from heat, stir in half the Gruyère and the Parmesan and season.
2 Pour one-third of the sauce into a bowl and stir in the pesto. Put a spoonful of sauce in the centre of each pancake, top with the chicken and artichokes, then fold in the sides of the pancakes and roll them up.
3 Arrange the pancakes in a single layer in a buttered shallow baking dish (about 25 cm x 30 cm/10 in x 12 in). Pour over the remaining sauce and scatter with Gruyère. Bake, uncovered, for 30 minutes or until the sauce is bubbling and golden.

• Per serving 730 kcalories, protein 48g, carbohydrate 38g, fat 44g, saturated fat 24g, fibre 2g, added sugar none, salt 2.08g

If you have time, marinate the chicken in the juice of half a lime for 10 minutes before cooking, to keep it tender.

Zesty Chicken with Cashews

2 tbsp clear honey
finely grated zest and juice of 2 limes
1 tsp vegetable oil
1 boneless skinless chicken breast,
cut into strips
50g/2oz roasted unsalted cashew
nuts
3 spring onions, sliced
150g pack straight-to-wok noodles
small handful of fresh coriander
leaves, roughly chopped

Takes 20 minutes • Serves 1

1 Whisk the honey and lime zest and juice in a small bowl. Heat the oil in a wok or non-stick frying pan over a high heat. Stir fry the chicken strips for 4–5 minutes until golden brown and almost cooked, then add the cashews and spring onions. Cook for 1 minute.

2 Separate the noodles into strands and toss into the wok with the lime and honey sauce, mixing well until heated through. Finally, stir in the coriander and serve immediately.

• Per serving 711 kcalories, protein 50g, carbohydrate 62g, fat 31g, saturated fat 4g, fibre 6g, sugar 4g, salt 0.25g

Perfect for a speedy supper on a warm summer's evening. If you want more time outdoors than in the kitchen, use four tablespoons of pesto from a jar, rather than making it yourself.

Summer Traybake Chicken

4 boneless skinless chicken breasts
1 tbsp olive oil
250g/9oz cherry tomatoes

FOR THE PESTO
50g/2oz pine nuts
1 large bunch fresh basil
50g/2oz Parmesan
150ml/¼ pint olive oil, plus extra for storing
2 garlic cloves, peeled

Takes 35 minutes • Serves 4

1 Make the pesto. Place a small frying pan over a low heat and dry fry the pine nuts until golden, shaking the pan occasionally. Put them in a food processor with the remaining ingredients and process until smooth, then season. Pour the pesto into a jar and cover with a little extra oil, then seal and store in the fridge for up to two weeks.
2 Put the chicken breasts in a large, shallow roasting tin and drizzle with the olive oil. Grill for 10 minutes then add the tomatoes and grill for another 5 minutes or until the chicken is cooked through. Drizzle four tablespoons of the pesto over the top and serve.

• Per serving 283 kcalories, protein 35.6g, carbohydrate 2.2g, fat 14.7g, saturated fat 2.7g, fibre 0.7g, sugar 2g, salt 0.29g

Noodles are the perfect accompaniment to this speedy stir fry.
Break 200g/8oz rice noodles into a large bowl, cover with boiling
water, leave for 4 minutes then drain and toss with a little sesame oil.

Summery Chicken Stir Fry

handful of cashew nuts
2 tbsp sunflower oil
2 boneless skinless chicken breasts,
cut into thin strips
3 spring onions, sliced
175g/6oz small broccoli florets
175g/6oz sugar snap peas, or
mangetout
½ small head Chinese leaves,
shredded
2 tbsp hoisin sauce

Takes 25 minutes • Serves 2

1 Heat a wok or large frying pan and dry fry
the cashews until toasted. Remove and set
aside. Heat one tablespoon of oil in the wok
and stir fry the chicken quickly until evenly
browned, then remove from the pan. Add the
remaining oil along with the spring onions and
broccoli and stir fry quickly for 2–3 minutes.
Add the peas and Chinese leaves and stir fry
for a further minute.
2 Return the chicken to the pan with the
hoisin sauce and six tablespoons of water.
Bring to the boil, then cover and cook for
5 minutes or until the chicken is cooked
through. Scatter over the nuts to serve.

• Per serving 420 kcalories, protein 45g, carbohydrate
16g, fat 20g, saturated fat 3g, fibre 6g, sugar 12g,
salt 0.78g

With just four ingredients, this low-fat grill recipe couldn't be simpler. Serve it with plain rice or potatoes and a green vegetable – broccoli or leeks would be good.

Lemon and Honey Chicken

4 chicken breasts, skin on
1 large lemon
2 tsp fresh thyme leaves, or a generous sprinkling of dried
1½ tbsp clear honey

Takes 20–30 minutes • Serves 4

1 Heat the grill to high and lightly oil a shallow flameproof dish. Put the chicken in the dish, skin-side down, and season with salt and pepper. Grill for 5 minutes. While the chicken is grilling, cut four thin slices from the lemon.

2 Turn the chicken over and put a slice of lemon on top of each breast. Sprinkle over the thyme and a little more seasoning, then drizzle with the honey. Squeeze over the juice from the remaining lemon and spoon around them two tablespoons of water. Return to the grill for 10 minutes more, or until the chicken is golden and cooked through.

• Per serving 193 kcalories, protein 33g, carbohydrate 6g, fat 4g, saturated fat 1g, fibre none, sugar 4g, salt 0.83g

A refreshing salad for a hot day, packed with vitamin C and folic acid.

Chicken and Orange Salad

150g pack green beans, trimmed
1 fennel bulb
1 large avocado
2 oranges
2 tbsp olive oil
100g bag watercress, roughly chopped
2 boneless skinless cooked chicken breasts, shredded

Takes 15 minutes • Serves 2

1 Cook the beans in a large pan of boiling salted water for 4–5 minutes. Drain and cool under the cold tap. Finely slice the fennel bulb, cutting away the core.

2 Halve the avocado and remove the stone, then peel and slice the flesh. Peel the oranges and cut out the segments. Squeeze the juice from the orange membranes into a large salad bowl and mix with the olive oil to make a dressing. Toss the prepared salad ingredients in the dressing with the watercress, pile into bowls and scatter the chicken on top before serving.

• Per serving 572 kcalories, protein 45g, carbohydrate 19g, fat 36g, saturated fat 5g, fibre 10g, sugar 17g, salt 0.30g

Although low in fat, this dish tastes rich, creamy and satisfying – comfort food without the guilt.

Chicken and Ham Chowder

1 tbsp sunflower oil
2 leeks, thinly sliced
3 potatoes, peeled and cut into small cubes
1 tbsp plain flour
700ml/1¼ pints skimmed milk
2 roasted chicken breasts, skinned and cut into chunks
2 thick slices of ham, chopped into chunks
175g/6oz frozen sweetcorn
175g/6oz frozen peas

Takes 30 minutes • Serves 4
(easily halved)

1 Heat the oil in a large pan and fry the leeks over a low heat for 3 minutes until softened. Stir in the potatoes and flour then slowly blend in the milk, stirring after each addition. Bring to the boil and simmer, uncovered, for 10–12 minutes until the potatoes are soft.
2 Add the chicken, ham, sweetcorn and peas and stir over a medium heat for 5 minutes or until hot and bubbling. Season to taste before serving.

• Per serving 341 kcalories, protein 34g, carbohydrate 37g, fat 7g, saturated fat 2g, fibre 5g, sugar 12g, salt 0.66g

A nutritious, low-fat feast that provides a satisfying four of your five-a-day. The chicken is a good source of protein and selenium, while the fennel is rich in B vitamins.

Chicken, Fennel and Tomato Ragout

1 large fennel bulb
1 tbsp olive oil
2 boneless skinless chicken breasts, cut into chunks
1 garlic clove, peeled and chopped
200g/8oz new potatoes, cut into chunks
400g can chopped tomatoes
150ml/¼ pint chicken or vegetable stock
3 roasted red peppers in brine, from a jar or deli counter, chopped
crusty bread, to serve

Takes 35 minutes • Serves 2 (easily doubled)

1 Trim the green tops off the fennel and reserve. Halve, then quarter the fennel, cut out the core, then cut lengthways into slices. Heat the oil in a pan, add the chicken and fry quickly until lightly coloured. Add the fennel and garlic, then stir briefly until the fennel is glistening.

2 Tip in the potatoes, tomatoes, stock and a little seasoning and bring to the boil. Cover and simmer for 20 minutes until the potatoes are tender. Stir in the peppers and heat through. Roughly chop the reserved fennel fronds and sprinkle them over the ragout. Serve with crusty bread to mop up the juices.

• Per serving 351 kcalories, protein 42g, carbohydrate 28g, fat 9g, saturated fat 1g, fibre 6g, sugar 10g, salt 1.43g

This tasty supper proves that low-fat, healthy food can be both flavoursome and satisfying.

Soy Steamed Chicken

2 boneless skinless chicken breasts, cut into chunks
1 tbsp reduced-salt soy sauce
1 tbsp sunflower oil
small knob of fresh root ginger, peeled and grated
3 spring onions, sliced
175g/6oz basmati rice
250g pack prepared vegetables, such as broccoli, carrots and green beans
425ml/¾ pint vegetable stock

Takes 30 minutes • Serves 2 (easily doubled)

1 Mix the chicken with the soy sauce and set aside. Heat the oil in a pan that has a well-fitting lid, add the ginger and onions and fry briefly. Stir in the rice and vegetables, pour in the stock and bring to the boil. Reduce the heat, cover and cook for 5 minutes, then put the chunks of chicken on top of the rice and pour over the soy-sauce marinade.
2 Re-cover the pan and cook for a further 12 minutes or until everything is tender and the chicken cooked through, then serve.

• Per serving 553 kcalories, protein 44g, carbohydrate 80g, fat 8g, saturated fat 1g, fibre 3g, sugar 8g, salt 1.33g

This magical salad gets flavour and texture from a few high-fat ingredients used sparingly, and still stays low in fat.

Warm Chicken and Avocado Salad

175g/6oz fine green beans, trimmed
1 tbsp sunflower seeds
2 tsp olive oil
4 boneless skinless chicken breasts, each sliced into about 8 pieces
1 romaine lettuce, trimmed and roughly sliced
1 bunch radishes, trimmed and sliced
1 small ripe avocado, stoned, peeled and sliced

FOR THE DRESSING
25g/1oz blue cheese, such as Danish blue or Saint Agur
100g/4oz low-fat fromage frais
2 tbsp semi-skimmed milk

Takes 20–30 minutes • Serves 4

1 Cook the beans in lightly salted water for 3–4 minutes until tender, yet still crisp. Cool under the cold tap, drain and set aside.

2 Tip the sunflower seeds into a large non-stick frying pan and swirl around for 1–2 minutes over a high heat until lightly toasted. Tip from the pan and set aside. Pour the olive oil into the pan and stir fry the chicken pieces over a high heat for 4–6 minutes until golden but still moist inside.

3 Meanwhile, make the dressing. Break up the blue cheese in a bowl, add the fromage frais and milk and mix until smooth. Season with black pepper.

4 Toss the beans and other vegetables together in a bowl then add the hot chicken and sunflower seeds. Serve warm, drizzled with the dressing.

• Per serving 292 kcalories, protein 40g, carbohydrate 6g, fat 12g, saturated fat 3g, fibre 3g, added sugar none, salt 0.5g

The clever use of a steamer makes this mouthwatering meal
a low-fat delight.

Chunky Chicken Hotpot

700ml/1¼ pints hot chicken stock
4 boneless skinless chicken breasts
100g/4oz smoked streaky bacon
rashers, chopped
½ small Savoy cabbage, cut into
4 wedges
6 carrots, peeled and cut into large
chunks

Takes 20 minutes • Serves 4

1 Pour the stock into the bottom of a
steamer then add the chicken and bacon. Sit
the cabbage and carrots in the first tier of the
steamer, above the stock mixture. Cover and
simmer for 15 minutes or until the chicken is
cooked through, the cabbage has wilted and
the carrots are tender.

2 Remove the chicken from the liquid and
slice each breast diagonally in half. Divide the
chicken, cabbage and carrots among four
bowls, then ladle over the stock and bacon
pieces. Serve hot.

• Per serving 332 kcalories, protein 47g, carbohydrate
15g, fat 10g, saturated fat 3g, fibre 6g, sugar 14g,
salt 2g

A vibrant and tasty dish that is low in fat. For an even healthier version, remove the skin from the chicken before serving.

Chicken with Beetroot and Watercress

2 tbsp sunflower oil
4 chicken breasts, skin on
400g jar baby beets in vinegar
3 tbsp clear honey
100g bag watercress

Takes 25 minutes • Serves 4

1 Heat the oil in a large frying pan over a medium heat. Season the chicken on both sides and fry, skin-side down, for 7 minutes until almost cooked through and the skin is crisp. Turn the chicken over, cook for another 3 minutes, then take out of the pan and keep warm on a plate.

2 Drain the beetroot, reserving the vinegar, and cut into wedges. Add the honey to the pan with three tablespoons of the vinegar then reduce to a syrupy glaze. Add the beets and any juices that have come out of the chicken on to the plate, then toss for a few minutes until hot.

3 Divide the watercress among four plates and top with the beetroot and chicken. Spoon the syrupy sauce over to serve.

• Per serving 282 kcalories, protein 34g, carbohydrate 16g, fat 10g, saturated fat 2g, fibre 2g, sugar 15g, salt 0.77g

This crunchy coleslaw is a great source of vitamin C and makes
a great light lunch.

Asian Chicken Coleslaw

300g/10oz red cabbage
1 large carrot, coarsely grated
1 red-skinned apple, coarsely grated
1 bunch spring onions,
thinly sliced
2 tbsp mayonnaise
1 tbsp white wine vinegar
2 tbsp extra virgin olive oil
1 large bunch basil, leaves torn
pinch of ground fenugreek
or ground coriander
finely grated zest and juice of 1 lime
4 boneless skinless chicken breasts

Takes 35 minutes • Serves 4

1 Using a large knife, shred the cabbage and place in a large bowl with the carrot, apple and spring onions. Whisk together the mayonnaise, vinegar and one tablespoon of the oil. Season then toss into the salad with half the basil.

2 Heat the grill to high. Chop the remaining basil and mix with the fenugreek, lime zest and juice, the remaining olive oil and seasoning. Rub the chicken breasts with the lime mix (leave to marinate for 10 minutes, if time), then grill for 6 minutes on each side or until golden and cooked through. Serve the chicken thickly sliced, on top of the coleslaw.

• Per serving 286 kcalories, protein 35g, carbohydrate 7g, fat 13g, saturated fat 2g, fibre 3g, sugar 6g, salt 0.34g

A mild, satisfying and low-fat curry that is tastier and healthier than a takeaway. Serve with plain rice and naan bread.

Light Chicken Korma

small knob of fresh root ginger, peeled and finely sliced
1 garlic clove, peeled and chopped
1 onion, sliced
1 tbsp vegetable oil
4 boneless skinless chicken breasts, cut into bite-sized pieces
1 tsp garam masala
100ml/3½fl oz hot chicken stock
3 tbsp low-fat fromage frais
2 tbsp ground almonds
handful of toasted, sliced almonds and fresh coriander sprigs, to serve

Takes 35 minutes • Serves 4

1 Cook the ginger, garlic and onion in a large pan with the oil until softened. Tip in the chicken and cook for about 5 minutes until lightly browned, then add the garam masala and cook for another minute.
2 Pour in the stock and simmer for 10 minutes or until the chicken is cooked through. Remove from the heat.
3 Mix the fromage frais and almonds together, then stir into the curry with the pan still off the heat. Garnish with sliced almonds and coriander, and serve with boiled rice and naan bread.

• Per serving 243 kcalories, protein 37g, carbohydrate 4g, fat 9g, saturated fat 1g, fibre 1g, sugar 3g, salt 0.31g

Use chicken thighs in this low-fat pilau, as they are cheaper than breasts and just as tasty; they also contain more iron. Chickpeas do their bit here and boost the fibre content.

Chicken, Broccoli and Chickpea Pilau

1 tbsp olive oil
4 chicken thighs, skinned and trimmed of fat
2 large leeks, thinly sliced
2 garlic cloves, peeled and crushed
400g can chickpeas in water, drained and rinsed
200g/8oz easy-cook brown rice
finely grated zest of 1 lemon
450ml/16fl oz hot chicken stock
1 head broccoli, broken into florets

Takes 40 minutes • Serves 4
(easily halved or doubled)

1 Heat the oil in a large flameproof casserole. Fry the chicken thighs for 2 minutes, turning halfway, until lightly coloured, then lift on to a plate. Add the leeks to the pan and stir fry for 3 minutes, then add the garlic and tip in the chickpeas and rice, and most of the lemon zest. Stir together until well mixed.

2 Nestle the chicken in the rice mix. Pour over the stock and season lightly. Cover and cook over a low heat for 20 minutes until the chicken is nearly cooked through and the rice has absorbed almost all of the liquid.

3 Sit the broccoli on top of the rice, cover and continue to cook until the rice and broccoli are tender and the chicken is cooked through. Sprinkle the remaining lemon zest on top before serving.

• Per serving 447 kcalories, protein 35g, carbohydrate 59g, fat 10g, saturated fat 2g, fibre 8g, sugar 4g, salt 0.8g

Packed with flavour, but low in carbs and fat, this dish is great in summer with rice and salad, or on colder days with mash broccoli.

Pesto Chicken

1 tbsp olive oil
4 boneless skinless chicken breasts
200g pack cherry tomatoes, halved
3 tbsp pesto
3 tbsp crème fraîche (full or half-fat)
fresh basil leaves (optional), to serve

Takes 25 minutes • Serves 4

1 Heat the oil in a frying pan, preferably non-stick. Add the chicken and fry without stirring until lightly coloured. Turn the chicken and fry on the other side. Continue frying for 12–15 minutes until the chicken is almost cooked. Season all over with a little salt and pepper.

2 Add the tomatoes to the pan, stirring them around for a couple of minutes until they start to soften. Reduce the heat and stir in the pesto and crème fraîche until it makes a sauce. Scatter with a few basil leaves.

• Per serving 262 kcalories, protein 37g, carbohydrate 2g, fat 12g, saturated fat 5g, fibre 1g, added sugar none, salt 0.37g

A fresh and light salad for a summer's day.

Balsamic Chicken and Peach Salad

2 tbsp balsamic vinegar
2 tbsp olive oil
4 boneless skinless chicken breasts
2 ripe peaches
100g/4oz baby spinach leaves
handful of fresh basil leaves

Takes 35 minutes • Serves 4

1 Heat the grill to medium and cover the rack with foil. Measure one tablespoon each of the vinegar and the oil into a shallow dish and add a good shake of salt and pepper. Add the chicken and turn in the dressing until well coated. Put the chicken in one layer on the grill rack and grill for 10–12 minutes, then turn the chicken over and grill for 10–12 minutes more or until cooked through, glossy and deep brown in colour.

2 Meanwhile, halve the peaches, remove the stones and slice the flesh fairly thickly. Spread the spinach over a serving platter. Slice the cooked chicken and scatter it over the spinach along with the peaches and half the basil. Shred the remaining basil and mix in a small bowl with the remaining vinegar and oil and seasoning. Drizzle over the salad and serve.

• Per serving 162 kcalories, protein 31g, carbohydrate 6g, fat 2g, saturated fat 1g, fibre 1g, added sugar none, salt 0.28g

Easy-to-make drumsticks that are delicious any time of year – ideal for a barbecue or just as good roasted in the oven.

Indian-style Drumsticks

8 chicken drumsticks, skinned

FOR THE MARINADE
142ml carton natural yoghurt
1 tbsp ground cumin
1 tbsp ground coriander
2 tsp turmeric
1 tsp chilli powder

Takes 25–30 minutes, plus marinating • Serves 4

1 With a sharp knife, make a few slashes in each drumstick. Mix the marinade ingredients in a bowl and season to taste. Add the drumsticks, rubbing the mixture into the meat well. Cover and marinate in the fridge for at least 30 minutes, or overnight.
2 Remove the drumsticks from the marinade, shaking off the excess. Barbecue for 20–25 minutes or until the chicken is cooked through, turning occasionally. Alternatively, roast for 30 minutes in an oven pre-heated to 200°C/Gas 6/fan 180°C.

• Per serving 229 kcalories, protein 37g, carbohydrate 6g, fat 7g, saturated fat 2g, fibre none, sugar 2g, salt 0.49g

An easy, low-fat dish using mainly store-cupboard ingredients
that make it perfect for an after-work supper.

Chicken Fried Rice

300g/10oz mixed basmati and
wild rice
1 chicken stock cube
4 boneless skinless chicken breasts,
thinly sliced
1 tbsp ground cumin
good pinch of chilli flakes
handful of fresh coriander leaves,
roughly chopped
1 tbsp sunflower oil
2 red peppers, seeded and
thinly sliced
400g can red kidney beans, drained
and rinsed
1 bunch spring onions,
thinly sliced

Takes 30 minutes • Serves 4

1 Put the rice in a pan, cover with water and crumble in the stock cube, then bring to the boil. Stir the rice once, then simmer for about 20 minutes until tender.

2 Meanwhile, toss the chicken in the spices and coriander. Heat the oil in a pan, tip in the peppers, and stir fry for 3 minutes until starting to soften. Add the chicken, then stir fry until golden and cooked through, about 5 minutes.

3 Drain the rice well and add to the chicken with the beans and spring onions. Toss together until hot then serve.

• Per serving 538 kcalories, protein 48g, carbohydrate 77g, fat 7g, saturated fat 1g, fibre 6g, sugar 8g, salt 1.91g

Using coconut milk in the marinade helps keep the chicken moist, without causing flames or smoke as oil can do. Serve on a bed of boiled rice tossed with chopped mint and coriander.

Red Curry Chicken Kebabs

2 boneless skinless chicken breasts, cut into large chunks
2 tbsp Thai red curry paste
2 tbsp coconut milk
1 red pepper, seeded and cut into chunks
1 courgette, halved and cut into chunks
1 red onion, peeled and cut into large chunks
lime wedges, to serve

Takes 20 minutes • Serves 2 (easily halved or doubled)

1 Fire up the barbecue or heat a griddle pan until hot. Tip the chicken, curry paste and coconut milk into a bowl, then mix well until the chicken is evenly coated.

2 Thread the vegetables and chicken on to skewers. Cook on the barbecue or griddle for 5–8 minutes or until the chicken is cooked through, turning the skewers occasionally. Serve with lime wedges for squeezing.

• Per kebab 251 kcalories, protein 36g, carbohydrate 10g, fat 8g, saturated fat 3g, fibre 2g, sugar 8g, salt 0.85g

This soup is packed with iron. Two types of lentils are used: the red ones break down and thicken the soup, while the green ones give a nutty texture.

Spiced Chicken and Lentil Soup

1 tsp each cumin and coriander seeds
1 tbsp sunflower oil
1 small onion, peeled and finely chopped
2 garlic cloves, peeled and finely chopped
14 curry leaves (freeze-dried or fresh)
½ tsp turmeric
1.3 litres/2¼ pints hot chicken stock
100g/4oz green lentils
100g/4oz red lentils
227g can chopped tomatoes
100g/4oz boneless skinless cooked chicken, cut into small cubes
150g carton natural yoghurt
good handful of fresh coriander leaves, chopped

Takes 40–45 minutes • Serves 4

1 Dry fry the cumin and coriander seeds in a small pan for 1–2 minutes until fragrant, then grind them using a pestle and mortar.

2 Heat the oil in a large pan, add the onion and fry for 3–4 minutes. Stir in the garlic and curry leaves, fry for a minute or until fragrant, then stir in the ground cumin and coriander and the turmeric. Pour in the stock and bring to the boil. Add the green lentils, lower the heat and simmer, uncovered, for 10 minutes. Stir in the red lentils and simmer for 15 minutes or until thickened.

3 Add the tomatoes and chicken and heat through. Stir in one tablespoon of the yoghurt and half the coriander. Mix the rest of the yoghurt and coriander together and serve separately, for swirling on top of the soup.

• Per serving 346 kcalories, protein 33g, carbohydrate 36g, fat 8g, saturated fat 2g, fibre 5g, sugar 8g, salt 0.91g

Bulghar is wheat that has been dehusked, cooked and dried then cracked into small pieces, and it makes a perfect foil for the spicy chicken. For a hotter version, use twice as much harissa.

Harissa Chicken with Bulghar

1 tbsp harissa paste
4 boneless skinless chicken breasts
1 tbsp vegetable or sunflower oil
1 onion, peeled, halved and sliced
2 tbsp pine nuts
handful of ready-to-eat dried apricots
300g/10oz bulghar
600ml/1 pint hot chicken stock
handful of fresh coriander leaves, chopped

Takes 30 minutes • Serves 4

1 Rub the harissa paste over the chicken. Heat the oil in a deep, non-stick pan, and fry the chicken for about 3 minutes on each side until just golden (it won't be cooked through at this stage). Remove and set aside.
2 Add the onion and fry gently for 5 minutes until soft. Toss in the pine nuts and continue cooking for another few minutes until toasted. Add the apricots, bulghar and stock, then season and cover. Cook for about 10 minutes until the stock is almost absorbed.
3 Return the chicken to the pan, re-cover and cook for 5 minutes over a low heat until the liquid has been absorbed and the chicken is cooked through. Fluff up the bulghar with a fork and scatter with the coriander to serve.

• Per serving 536 kcalories, protein 49g, carbohydrate 65g, fat 11g, saturated fat 2g, fibre 2g, sugar 8g, salt 1.06g

A light and spicy take on Cornish pasties, these are equally good served hot or cold.

Spicy Chicken and Bacon Pasties

2 rashers streaky bacon, chopped
1 large potato (about 250g/8oz), peeled and cut into small cubes
1 small red chilli, seeded and finely chopped
1 boneless skinless cooked chicken breast, shredded
3 spring onions, thinly sliced
375g pack ready-rolled puff pastry
2 tbsp milk

Takes 30 minutes • Serves 4

1 Fry the bacon in a non-stick pan for a few minutes until the fat runs. Add the potato, increase the heat and fry for 5 minutes, stirring occasionally, until the bacon is crisp and potato just underdone. Add the chilli and cook for a minute. Season to taste, then tip into a bowl with the chicken and onions.
2 Pre-heat the oven to 220°C/Gas 7/fan 200°C. Re-roll the pastry until large enough to cut out four discs (use a large saucer or side plate as a guide). Put on a baking sheet.
3 Spoon the filling on to the centre of each disc. Brush the edges of the pastry with a little milk, then bring them up to the middle and pinch at the top to make a pasty. Brush the pasties all over with milk, then bake for 15 minutes or until golden.

• Per serving 439 kcalories, protein 17g, carbohydrate 42g, fat 24g, saturated fat 9g, fibre 1g, sugar 2g, salt 1.06g

Any leftovers from this one-pot rice dish can be used for a salad up to two days later. Mix with mayonnaise and a squeeze of fresh lemon juice and serve with Little Gem lettuce and sliced cucumber.

Chicken Biryani

300g/10oz basmati rice
25g/1oz butter
1 large onion, peeled and finely sliced
1 bay leaf
3 cardamom pods
1 small cinnamon stick
1 tsp turmeric
4 boneless skinless chicken breasts, cut into large chunks
4 tbsp curry paste
85g/3oz raisins
850ml/1½ pints hot chicken stock
small handful each of chopped fresh coriander leaves and toasted flaked almonds, to serve

Takes 40 minutes • Serves 4

1 Soak the rice in warm water, then wash in cold until the water runs clear. Heat the butter in a pan and cook the onion with the bay leaf and whole spices for 10 minutes. Sprinkle in the turmeric, add the chicken and curry paste and cook until aromatic.

2 Stir the rice into the pan with the raisins, then pour over the stock. Place a tight-fitting lid on the pan and bring to a hard boil, then lower the heat to a minimum and cook the rice for another 5 minutes. Turn off the heat and leave for 10 minutes.

3 To serve, mix through some of the coriander then top with the rest of the coriander and the almonds.

• Per serving 617 kcalories, protein 49g, carbohydrate 83g, fat 12g, saturated fat 4g, fibre 2g, sugar 19g, salt 2.01g

A simple meal that looks as good as it tastes. If you don't like your food too hot and spicy, use a milder curry paste.

Couscous with Chicken and Apricots

250g/8oz couscous
300ml/½ pint hot chicken stock
3 tbsp olive oil
1 onion, peeled and chopped
2 large boneless skinless chicken breasts, sliced
85g/3oz blanched almonds
1 tbsp hot curry paste
100g/4oz ready-to-eat dried apricots, halved
20g pack fresh coriander, leaves chopped
natural yoghurt, to serve (optional)

Takes 20–30 minutes • Serves 4

1 Put the couscous in a large bowl and stir in the stock. Cover the bowl with cling film and leave to stand.
2 Heat the oil in a pan and cook the onion for 2–3 minutes until softened. Toss in the chicken and stir fry for 5–6 minutes until tender and just cooked through. Add the almonds and, when golden, stir in the curry paste and cook for 1 minute more.
3 Fluff up the couscous grains with a fork, then add to the chicken with the apricots and coriander. Toss until hot, then serve with yoghurt, if you like.

• Per serving 486 kcalories, protein 28g, carbohydrate 45g, fat 23g, saturated fat 2g, fibre 4g, added sugar none, salt 0.56g

Creamed coconut is an excellent ingredient to have on standby in the fridge. It is sold in blocks, so you can cut off a piece when you need it or simply grate it directly into food.

Aromatic Chicken Curry

100g/4oz creamed coconut, roughly chopped
2 tbsp vegetable oil
1 large onion, peeled and chopped
4 tsp garam masala
1 small cinnamon stick
2–3 tsp hot chilli powder, to taste
8 boneless skinless chicken thighs
handful of fresh coriander leaves
naan bread, to serve

Takes 40 minutes • Serves 4
(easily doubled)

1 Dissolve the creamed coconut in 500ml/18fl oz boiling water. Heat the oil in a deep frying pan and fry the onion gently for about 10 minutes until softened and light golden. Add the spices and chicken then fry for 2 minutes, stirring to coat the meat.

2 Pour the coconut milk into the pan and stir well. Season with salt and bring to the boil, then simmer for 20 minutes or until the chicken is cooked through and the sauce has thickened. Sprinkle with the coriander and serve with naan.

• Per serving 380 kcalories, protein 40g, carbohydrate 9g, fat 21g, saturated fat 10g, fibre 1g, sugar 5g, salt 0.5g

You can find quinoa in many supermarkets and health-food shops, or you can substitute it with rice. Simply boil 300g/10oz long grain rice and use in the same way as the quinoa.

Moroccan Chicken with Quinoa

4 boneless skinless chicken breasts
finely grated zest and juice of
1 lemon
2 tbsp olive oil
4 tsp Moroccan spice mix
300g/10oz quinoa
1 bunch spring onions, chopped
handful of green olives, pitted and
halved
1 small bunch fresh flatleaf parsley,
leaves chopped

Takes 30 minutes • Serves 4
(easily halved or doubled)

1 Pre-heat the oven to 180°C/Gas 4/fan 160°C. Cut three deep slashes in each chicken breast and place in a baking dish. Mix the lemon zest, juice, oil and spices together then pour over the chicken. Cover with foil and bake for 20 minutes.
2 Meanwhile, cook the quinoa according to the packet instructions then tip it into a large bowl. Stir through the rest of the ingredients and divide among four serving plates. Remove the chicken from the oven, cut each piece into three and serve on top of the quinoa, with the juices drizzled over.

• Per serving 461 kcalories, protein 45g, carbohydrate 45g, fat 12g, saturated fat 1g, fibre 1g, sugar 6g, salt 2.11g

A make-ahead meal that will keep in the fridge for up to two days. Reheat in a covered casserole for 20 minutes or until bubbling (stir in a splash of water if the sauce is too thick).

Cumin-scented Chicken Curry

4 tbsp vegetable oil
2 tsp cumin seeds
2 onions, peeled and sliced
3cm/1in piece fresh root ginger, peeled and shredded
3 fat garlic cloves, shredded
3 plump green chillies, halved lengthways (seeded for a milder curry)
½ tsp turmeric
½ tsp garam masala
2 tsp paprika
12 large skinless chicken thighs, bone in
2 large peppers (1 red and 1 yellow or orange), seeded and cut into rough chunks
2 tbsp tomato purée
250g carton natural yoghurt
3 tbsp chopped fresh coriander

Takes 40–50 minutes • Serves 6

1 Heat the oil in a large wok over a low heat and fry the cumin for a few seconds until fragrant. Add the onions, cover and cook for 10 minutes until soft but not coloured.
2 Scatter in the ginger, garlic and chillies and fry for a minute, then sprinkle in the ground spices and stir in the chicken and peppers. Fry for 10 minutes until the onions turn russet brown, adding a splash of water if they start to catch on the bottom of the pan.
3 Stir the tomato purée into the yoghurt and swirl into the pan, followed by 125ml/4fl oz cold water. Simmer gently without a lid for 30–35 minutes or until the chicken is cooked through, stirring in a little more water if the sauce becomes dry – it should thicken and take on a reddish tinge. Add salt if you wish. Scatter over the coriander before serving.

• Per serving 810 kcalories, protein 60g, carbohydrate 11g, fat 59g, saturated fat 16g, fibre 2g, added sugar none, salt 0.76g

A fabulously quick dish that's ideal for after-school. The chicken is slashed, to help the topping stay on and to allow the heat to penetrate the meat more quickly.

Chicken Nacho Grills

40g bag tortilla chips
4 boneless skinless chicken breasts
200g carton fresh spicy tomato salsa
142ml carton soured cream
handful of grated mature Cheddar

Takes 20–25 minutes • Serves 4

1 Pre-heat the oven to 200°C/Gas 6/fan 180°C. Crush the tortilla chips. Put the chicken in a roasting tin (preferably non-stick) and slash each breast three times with a sharp knife. Season, then spoon one tablespoon of salsa on top of each breast followed by one tablespoon of soured cream.
2 Sprinkle the chips over the chicken, and top with the grated cheese. Roast for 15–20 minutes or until the topping is golden and the chicken cooked through then serve.

• Per serving 326 kcalories, protein 39g, carbohydrate 12g, fat 14g, saturated fat 7g, fibre 1g, sugar 4g, salt 1.91g

A simple and superhealthy all-in-one dish that is an ideal mid-week supper for all the family.

Oven-baked Chicken Pilau

85g/3oz pine nuts
2 tbsp olive oil
1 red onion, peeled and cut into thin wedges
1 tsp turmeric
good pinch of dried chilli flakes
8 boneless skinless chicken thighs
350g/12oz long grain rice
85g/3oz sultanas
850ml/1½ pints hot chicken stock
handful of fresh coriander leaves, to serve

Takes 30 minutes • Serves 4

1 Pre-heat the oven to 200°C/Gas 6/fan 180°C. On the hob, dry fry the pine nuts in a flameproof casserole until toasted. Remove and set aside.
2 Heat the oil in the casserole and soften the onion with the turmeric and chilli for 3 minutes. Add the chicken pieces and cook for 3–4 minutes until browned all over. Tip in the rice, sultanas and 750ml/1¼ pints of the stock, and bring to the boil. Cover with a lid and transfer to the oven for 20 minutes, or until the chicken is cooked through and the rice is tender. Check halfway and add more stock if needed. Season to taste, then stir in the toasted pine nuts and sprinkle with coriander to serve.

• Per serving 784 kcalories, protein 48g, carbohydrate 95g, fat 26g, saturated fat 4g, fibre 1g, sugar 17g, salt 1.14g

A fragrant, gingery twist on a traditional curry. Serve with pilau rice, mango chutney and some poppadoms or naan bread.

Ginger Chicken

1kg pack boneless skinless chicken thighs, sliced into chunks
2 onions, peeled and quartered
1 tbsp sunflower oil
1 tsp turmeric
400ml can reduced-fat coconut milk
1 fresh red chilli, seeded and sliced
1 chicken stock cube

FOR THE MARINADE
knob of fresh root ginger, peeled and very finely chopped
4 garlic cloves, peeled and finely chopped
1 tsp mild chilli powder
juice of 1 lime
1 tbsp sunflower oil
15g pack fresh coriander leaves, chopped

Takes 50 minutes, plus marinating
Serves 6

1 Put the chicken in a bowl with the ginger, garlic, chilli powder, lime juice, oil and half the coriander. Mix well, cover and marinate in the fridge overnight.
2 Finely chop the onions in a food processor. Heat the oil in a wok and fry the onions for 8 minutes or until soft. Add the turmeric and stir fry for a minute. Tip in the chicken and marinade and cook until the chicken changes colour. Pour in the coconut milk, add the fresh chilli, crumble in the stock cube and bring to the boil. Cover and simmer for 20 minutes or until the chicken is cooked through. Sprinkle the remaining coriander on top just before serving.

• Per serving 310 kcalories, protein 37g, carbohydrate 6g, fat 16g, saturated fat 8g, fibre 1g, sugar 3g, salt 1.29g

To give these noodles an extra Asian touch, add a handful of torn mint leaves and finely sliced cucumber at the end of cooking.

Chicken Pot Noodles

500ml/18fl oz hot chicken or vegetable stock
400ml can coconut milk (full- or reduced-fat)
1 tbsp Thai green or red curry paste
1 tsp turmeric
3 boneless skinless chicken breasts, sliced
250g pack medium rice noodles
300g bag vegetable stir-fry mix (including beansprouts)

Takes 15–20 minutes • Serves 4

1 Tip the stock, coconut milk, curry paste, turmeric and chicken into a large microwave-proof bowl. Cover with cling film and pierce a few times, then microwave on High for 5 minutes. Remove the cling film, give everything a good stir and microwave on High again for a further 5 minutes until the chicken is tender and cooked through.

2 Meanwhile, pour boiling water over the noodles in another large bowl and leave to soak for 4 minutes.

3 Drain the noodles and add to the chicken with the stir-fry mix. Stir well, ladle into deep bowls and serve.

• Per serving 516 kcalories, protein 32g, carbohydrate 58g, fat 19g, saturated fat 14g, fibre 1g, added sugar none, salt 1.03g

A healthy supper dish, but if you're not counting calories and you want to make it more substantial, top it with mash and grill until heated through and crisp on top.

Crisp Chicken and Asparagus Pie

4 boneless skinless chicken breasts, cut into bite-sized pieces
knob of butter
100g/4oz asparagus, cut into bite-sized pieces
100g/4oz green vegetables (baby spinach and fresh or frozen peas)
100g/4oz cooked ham, torn
100ml/3½ fl oz low-fat crème fraîche
50g/2oz fresh breadcrumbs

Takes 20 minutes • Serves 4

1 Heat the grill to medium. Spread the chicken out evenly in a shallow flameproof dish. Dot with a little butter and grill for 7–10 minutes, turning occasionally until cooked through. Meanwhile, put the vegetables in a bowl and pour boiling water over them. Leave for 2–3 minutes, then drain.
2 Scatter the vegetables and ham over the chicken, then top with the crème fraîche and season to taste. Sprinkle over the breadcrumbs, dot with the remaining butter, then slide under the grill for 5 minutes or until the topping is crisp.

• Per serving 300 kcalories, protein 43g, carbohydrate 13g, fat 9g, saturated fat 5g, fibre 1g, added sugar none, salt 1.21g

This salad has a delicious Mexican influence, combining warm chicken tossed with cumin and chilli, kidney beans and creamy avocado.

Cumin Chicken and Avocado Salad

2 tbsp olive oil
1 heaped tsp ground cumin
1 heaped tsp mild chilli powder
4 boneless skinless chicken breasts
400g pack cherry tomatoes, halved if large
1 red onion, peeled and finely chopped
4 Little Gem lettuce hearts, separated into leaves
20g pack fresh coriander, leaves roughly chopped
3 Hass avocados, peeled and thickly sliced
6 tbsp bottled Caesar dressing
400g can red kidney beans, drained and rinsed

Takes 20 minutes • Serves 4

1 Mix the oil and spices in a large bowl, then use the mixture to coat the chicken. Pan fry the chicken (without extra oil) in a large non-stick frying pan for a few minutes on each side. Toss the tomatoes into any spiced oil left in the bowl, then add to the pan. Cover and cook for 5 minutes more, or until the chicken is cooked through and the tomatoes are warm and starting to soften.

2 Meanwhile, toss the onion, lettuce, coriander and avocados in the dressing and pile on to a large platter. Top with small handfuls of the beans and scatter with the tomatoes. Slice the warm chicken and pile on top.

• Per serving 636 kcalories, protein 43g, carbohydrate 22g, fat 43g, saturated fat 4g, fibre 10g, sugar 9g, salt 0.88g

To keep the combination of textures and flavours strong in this stir fry, add the watercress at the last moment so that it wilts only slightly and keeps its crunch.

Watercress and Chicken Stir Fry

1 tbsp sunflower oil
2 boneless skinless chicken breasts,
cut into strips
100g/4oz cashew nuts
1 yellow or red pepper, seeded
and chopped into large chunks
1 red onion, peeled and chopped
into large chunks
2 x 75g bags watercress
boiled rice, to serve

FOR THE SAUCE
3 tbsp hoisin sauce
2 tbsp soy sauce
large knob fresh root ginger,
peeled and finely grated
2 garlic cloves, peeled and crushed
1 tbsp sesame oil
2 tbsp rice wine vinegar or white
wine vinegar

Takes 20 minutes • Serves 4

1 To make the sauce, mix all the ingredients together in a small bowl until they are completely blended.
2 Heat the oil in a frying pan until very hot. Throw in the chicken, cashew nuts, pepper and onion and stir fry for about 4–5 minutes or until the chicken is cooked through and the nuts are toasted.
3 Pour over the sauce and simmer with a splash of water. Remove the pan from the heat, and stir in the watercress. Serve straight away, with boiled rice.

• Per serving 323 kcalories, protein 24g, carbohydrate 15g, fat 19g, saturated fat 2g, fibre 3g, sugar 10g, salt 1.92g

A mouthwatering mix of zesty flavours makes this the perfect light supper on a warm evening.

Sticky Chicken with Mango Couscous

1 large mango
4 spring onions, thinly sliced on the diagonal
1 heaped tsp ground cumin
3 tbsp white wine vinegar
250g/9oz couscous
3 tbsp thick-cut marmalade
4 tsp grainy mustard
4 boneless skinless chicken breasts, each sliced into 3–4 strips

Takes 20 minutes • Serves 4

1 Heat the grill to high. Peel and dice the mango, toss with most of the spring onions, the cumin and white wine vinegar, then set aside. Put the couscous in a large heatproof bowl, stir in 400ml/14fl oz boiling water, then cover with cling film and set aside.
2 Mix the marmalade and mustard together. Lay the chicken strips in a roasting tin and brush with half the marmalade glaze. Grill for 4–5 minutes, then turn the chicken over and brush with the remaining glaze. Grill for a further 4–5 minutes or until the chicken is cooked through and the glaze is bubbling.
3 Fluff up the couscous with a fork and stir in the mango mixture. Top with the chicken strips and the remaining spring onions and serve while it's hot.

• Per serving 369 kcalories, protein 35g, carbohydrate 53g, fat 3g, saturated fat 1g, fibre 3g, sugar 21g, salt 0.43g

Using tapenade makes this a speedy dish, but if you don't have any, chop up 12 pitted black olives and mix with a splash of olive oil. Or replace the tapenade with pesto or sun-dried tomato paste.

Tapenade Chicken on Ciabatta

1 ciabatta roll, cut in half
1 boneless skinless chicken breast
2 tsp tapenade (olive paste)
1 large tomato, thickly sliced
½ garlic clove
olive oil, to drizzle
handful of rocket leaves, to garnish

Takes 10 minutes • Serves 1
(easily doubled)

1 Griddle the ciabatta halves, cut-side down. Meanwhile, slice the chicken into 5–6 slivers, cutting across the width of the breast at an angle, rather than straight down, then toss in the tapenade. Remove the bread from the pan, add the chicken and tomato slices and leave to cook.

2 Rub the toasted bread with the cut side of the garlic, to give it a light flavour. Flip the chicken and tomatoes over – the chicken should only take about 5 minutes in total. Drizzle the garlicky bread with olive oil and top with the tomatoes, chicken and rocket leaves.

• Per serving 596 kcalories, protein 44g, carbohydrate 51g, fat 25g, saturated fat 3g, fibre 4g, sugar 8g, salt 1.72g

A simple yet sensational low-fat supper that's packed with flavour and vitamin C.

Chicken with Orange and Avocado Salsa

2 tsp olive oil
4 boneless skinless chicken breasts, cut diagonally in half
finely grated zest and juice of 1 lime
1 ripe avocado
2 oranges
1 red chilli, seeded and diced (optional)
3 spring onions, finely sliced
1 tbsp chopped fresh coriander or basil leaves

Takes 20 minutes • Serves 4

1 Heat the oil in a non-stick frying pan, season the chicken and fry for 10 minutes, turning once. Add the lime zest and juice for the final minute of cooking.

2 Meanwhile, halve the avocado and remove the stone. Peel away the skin and cut the flesh into small chunks. Tip into a bowl. Cut away the skin and pith of the oranges, cut out the segments, then add to the avocado with the remaining ingredients. Toss together gently, then serve alongside the chicken.

• Per serving 240 kcalories, protein 35g, carbohydrate 8g, fat 8g, saturated fat 1g, fibre 3g, sugar 7g, salt 0.23g

This dish makes unashamed use of quick-cook ingredients to create a tasty and appetizing stir fry in just 15 minutes.

Quick Chicken Noodles

1 tbsp sunflower or vegetable oil
4 boneless skinless chicken thighs, diced
1 garlic clove, peeled and crushed or sliced
1 red pepper, seeded and thinly sliced
1 small bunch spring onions, sliced
100g/4oz beansprouts
2 x 150g packs straight-to-wok noodles
3 tbsp oyster sauce

Takes 15 minutes • Serves 2
(easily halved or doubled)

1 Heat the oil in a large frying pan. Cook the chicken for about 3 minutes, or until golden.
2 Throw in the garlic and pepper and cook for 2 minutes more. Next, add the spring onions, beansprouts, noodles, sauce and five tablespoons of water and toss everything together to cook for a final 2 minutes. Serve immediately.

• Per serving 441 kcalories, protein 31g, carbohydrate 55g, fat 12g, saturated fat 2g, fibre 5g, sugar 11g, salt 4.07g

To make this salad no-cook, shred four cooked chicken breasts and add the olives, salad leaves and onion. Whisk together the lemon zest and juice, thyme, oil and garlic paste. Season and drizzle over.

Lemon and Thyme Chicken Salad

4 boneless skinless chicken breasts, cut into strips
finely grated zest and juice of 1 lemon
1 tsp dried thyme or a few fresh thyme sprigs
3 tbsp vegetable oil
150g bag mixed salad leaves or 2 Little Gem lettuces, pulled apart
1 small red onion, peeled and halved and thinly sliced
squeeze of garlic paste or 1 garlic clove, peeled and crushed
handful of pitted black olives, halved

Takes 20 minutes • Serves 4

1 Put the chicken pieces into a bowl and add the lemon zest, thyme, plenty of black pepper and salt to taste, then mix well with your hands. Heat one tablespoon of the oil in a pan and fry the chicken for 8–10 minutes, or until golden and cooked through. Meanwhile, spread the leaves and onion over a large platter or in a salad bowl.
2 Add the garlic paste and olives to the pan, then fry for 1 minute more. Spoon the chicken and olives on to the leaves. Take the pan off the heat and stir in the rest of the oil and the lemon juice. Stir together well, scraping up any bits from the bottom of the pan. Check the seasoning, pour over the chicken and salad, and serve.

• Per serving 245 kcalories, protein 34g, carbohydrate 2g, fat 11g, saturated fat 2g, fibre 1g, sugar 2g, salt 0.72g

These wraps can also be made Thai-style – with sweet chilli or lime and coriander chicken pieces instead of tikka, and a drizzle of sweet chilli sauce to serve.

Chicken Tikka Wraps

¼ cucumber, halved lengthways and sliced
¼ iceberg lettuce, shredded
2 spring onions, sliced
handful of fresh mint leaves, torn
4 small plain naan breads
140g pack cooked chicken tikka pieces
8 tbsp natural yoghurt

Takes 15 minutes • Serves 4

1 Toss all the salad vegetables and the mint together. Heat the naan in the microwave on Medium for 1 minute until puffed up. Remove and keep warm.
2 Tip the tikka pieces into a bowl and give them a quick blast in the microwave to heat through. Split the breads in half and stuff with salad, chicken and a tablespoon of yoghurt.

• Per serving 242 kcalories, protein 16.7g, carbohydrate 33.4g, fat 5.5g, saturated fat 2.3g, fibre 1.7g, sugar 4.8g, salt 1.04g

Chicken at its best: delicately flavoured, easy to cook and low in fat. The perfect ingredients for a simple summer supper.

Griddled Chicken with Lemon and Thyme

4 boneless skinless chicken breasts
finely grated zest of 1 lemon
2 tbsp fresh lemon juice
2 tbsp extra virgin olive oil, plus extra
for drizzling
2 garlic cloves, peeled and crushed
¼ tsp dried thyme

TO SERVE
houmous
kalamata olives
salad leaves
bread

Takes 20 minutes • Serves 4

1 Mix the chicken breasts with the lemon zest and juice, the olive oil, garlic and thyme. Season then cook on a heated griddle pan or the barbecue for 4–5 minutes on each side.
2 Serve the chicken hot, drizzled with olive oil. Accompany with generous spoonfuls of houmous, plus olives, salad and bread.

• Per serving 201 kcalories, protein 34g, carbohydrate 1g, fat 7g, saturated fat 1g, fibre none, added sugar none, salt 0.21g

This no-cook salad makes the ideal quick supper and is just as good for a lunchbox.

Minty Asian Chicken Salad

250g pack thin rice noodles
2 cooked chicken breasts, skinned and shredded
½ cucumber, halved lengthways and sliced
3 spring onions, sliced
1 red chilli, finely chopped (with or without seeds, according to taste)
4 tbsp soy or fish sauce
finely grated zest and juice of 1 lime
2 tsp sugar (any type)
20g pack fresh mint, leaves roughly chopped

Takes 10 minutes • Serves 4

1 Soak the noodles for 5 minutes in boiling water or according to the packet instructions until softened. Drain, then cool under a cold running tap. Drain again well, then tip into a large bowl along with the chicken, cucumber, spring onions and chilli.

2 Mix together the soy or fish sauce, lime zest and juice and the sugar and pour it over the noodles. Toss through the mint leaves and serve.

• Per serving 320 kcalories, protein 22g, carbohydrate 56g, fat 2g, saturated fat 1g, fibre none, sugar 5g, salt 2.83

For a subtle twist, use ginger marmalade with the zest and juice of a small orange. For added heat, add a pinch of chilli flakes. Serve with rice or mash to mop up the sauce, plus a fresh green salad.

Marmalade-glazed Chicken

4 boneless skinless chicken breasts
1 tbsp olive oil
300ml/½ pint hot chicken stock
4 tbsp fine-cut marmalade
1 tsp fresh thyme leaves or
½ tsp dried

Takes 15–20 minutes • Serves 4

1 Season the chicken, if you like. Heat the oil in a deep frying pan and fry the chicken for about 8 minutes until golden on each side, turning once. Add the stock, marmalade and thyme, stir well to mix then simmer for 5 minutes, spooning the sauce over the chicken as it cooks.

2 Remove the chicken and boil the sauce hard until reduced to a syrup. Return the chicken to the pan and turn the pieces in the sauce until they become glazed. Serve hot.

• Per serving 215 kcalories, protein 34g, carbohydrate 11g, fat 4g, saturated fat 1g, fibre none, sugar 9g, salt 0.50g

To make this warm salad gluten-free, replace the couscous with 200g/8oz long grain rice that has been cooked and cooled.

Lemon Chicken with Couscous

4 ready-roast chicken breasts, skinned and sliced
finely grated zest and juice of 1 lemon
3 tbsp olive oil
300g/10oz couscous
400ml/14fl oz hot chicken stock
250g pack cherry tomatoes, halved
50g/2oz toasted pine nuts, almonds or walnuts
large handful of fresh mint leaves, roughly torn

Takes 20 minutes • Serves 4 (easily halved)

1 Place the chicken in a shallow dish. Whisk the lemon zest and juice with the olive oil and seasoning then pour over the chicken. Cover and set aside.

2 Put the couscous in a bowl and stir in the hot stock. Cover the bowl with cling film and leave until the stock is absorbed, about 10 minutes. Fluff up with a fork then fold in the tomatoes, nuts and half the mint. Drain the marinade from the chicken and mix two-thirds of it into the couscous. Taste for seasoning.

3 Pile the chicken on top of the couscous, drizzle over the remaining marinade and top with the rest of the mint.

• Per serving 537 kcalories, protein 45g, carbohydrate 41g, fat 22g, saturated fat 4g, fibre 1g, added sugar none, salt 0.6g.

Don't let the simplicity of this quick-fix salad deceive you –
it's a meal in itself.

Chicken and Pepper Salad Bowl

1 whole ready-roast chicken, skinned
and torn into bite-sized pieces
85g pack prosciutto or Serrano ham,
torn into large pieces
180g bag Continental salad leaves
(lollo rosso, frisée, lamb's lettuce,
oak leaf, etc)
3 roasted red peppers from a jar,
cut into strips

FOR THE DRESSING
150g carton low-fat natural yogurt
juice of 1 lemon
1 garlic clove, peeled and crushed

Takes 15 minutes • Serves 4

1 Make the dressing. Whisk the yoghurt,
lemon juice and garlic together in a large
salad bowl. Season, then set aside for
at least 5 minutes to allow the flavours
to develop.
2 Tip the chicken, ham, salad leaves and
red peppers into the bowl then toss with
the dressing until all the ingredients are
evenly coated.

• Per serving 467 kcalories, protein 57g, carbohydrate
7g, fat 24g, saturated fat 6g, fibre 2g, added sugar
none, salt 2.37g

Stir fries are perfect for a meal in a hurry. This one is ultra-quick and low fat, and so full of fresh flavours you'll think twice about reaching for the take-away menu again.

Chilli Chicken with Honey and Soy

½ x 250g pack rice noodles
1 tbsp olive oil
275g/9½oz boneless skinless chicken breast, diced
1 red pepper, seeded and sliced
½ bunch spring onions (about 6), trimmed and halved crossways
½ tsp red chilli spice blend (chopped fresh chilli in a tube)
3 tbsp soy sauce, preferably dark
1 tbsp clear honey
5 Savoy cabbage leaves, sliced into thick strips
small handful of fresh coriander leaves, roughly chopped

Takes 20 minutes • Serves 2

1 Pour boiling water over the rice noodles in a bowl and leave to soak.
2 Heat the oil in a wok, add the chicken and stir fry for a few minutes until the pieces start to turn white. Throw in the pepper and the white halves of the onions and stir again – by now the chicken should be white all over.
3 Stir the chilli, soy and honey into the wok, then pile the cabbage on top and cover the wok with a lid. Cook for a few minutes until the chicken is tender then toss in the green spring-onion halves and the coriander. Stir well and serve with the drained rice noodles.

• Per serving 532 kcalories, protein 52g, carbohydrate 67g, fat 8g, saturated fat 1g, fibre 4g, sugar 6g, salt 4.4g

Less fat, less guilt but just as much flavour in these burgers, and toasted breadcrumbs are a clever short cut and low-fat alternative to getting golden crumbs by frying.

Chicken Burgers with Lemon Mayo

4 boneless skinless chicken breasts
3 slices white bread, toasted
1 egg
1 tsp Dijon mustard
finely grated zest of 1 lemon
juice of ½ lemon
4 tbsp reduced-fat mayonnaise
4 ciabatta rolls, halved and warmed
or toasted
salad, to serve

Takes 20 minutes • Serves 4

1 Heat the grill to high. Put the chicken breasts between two pieces of cling film and pound with a rolling pin until they are about half their original thickness. Whiz the toast in a food processor to rough breadcrumbs, then tip on to a plate.

2 Beat the egg and mustard in a bowl and season. Dip the chicken into the egg, let the excess drip back into the bowl, then press into the toasted breadcrumbs. Put under the grill on a flat baking sheet and grill for 10 minutes, turning once, until the chicken is cooked through and crisp on both sides.

3 Beat the lemon zest, juice and lots of black pepper into the mayonnaise. Spread some of the mayonnaise over the bottom halves of the rolls, pile on a chicken breast each and salad, then top with bun lids.

• Per serving 396 kcalories, protein 43g, carbohydrate 37g, fat 10g, saturated fat 2g, fibre 2g, sugar 2g, salt 1.8g

If you're watching your fat intake, remove the skin from the chicken breast before serving, but leave it on while it's cooking as it adds flavour and ensures the meat doesn't dry out.

Warm Chicken Salad

2 boneless chicken breasts, cut into bite-sized pieces
½ small baguette, cut into bite-sized pieces
4 tbsp olive oil
1 tbsp balsamic vinegar
150g pack mixed salad leaves
250g pack cooked beetroot, cut into bite-sized pieces
100g/4oz goats' cheese, crumbled

Takes 20 minutes • Serves 2

1 Pre-heat the oven to 200°C/Gas 6/fan 180°C. Spread the chunks of chicken and baguette over a shallow roasting tin. Drizzle with two tablespoons of the olive oil and toss to coat. Season, then put in the oven for 15 minutes, or until the chicken is cooked through and the bread is golden and crisp. Meanwhile, whisk the remaining oil with the vinegar in a jug to make a dressing.
2 Toss the warm chicken and bread with the salad leaves, and divide between two plates. Scatter the beetroot and cheese over the top, drizzle with the dressing, and serve straight away.

• Per serving 625 kcalories, protein 48g, carbohydrate 32g, fat 35g, saturated fat 10g, fibre 4g, sugar 15g, salt 2.88g

The easy, Asian-inspired glaze in this dish really peps up a simple chicken breast. It's already low fat, but if you want to reduce the calorie count further, remove the skin from the chicken before serving.

Sweet Chilli Chicken

3–4 tbsp chilli sauce, to taste
2 tbsp clear honey
2 tbsp olive oil
4 boneless chicken breasts, skin on
2 garlic cloves, peeled and crushed
lime wedges, to serve (optional)

Takes 20 minutes • Serves 4

1 Heat the grill to high. Mix together the chilli sauce, honey and oil in a large bowl to make a glaze. Using a sharp knife, make 3–4 slits across the skin side of each chicken breast. Season with salt and pepper, if you like, then lift the skin on each breast and tuck under the crushed garlic. Dip the underside of each breast in the glaze until evenly coated. Reserve the rest of the glaze for later.
2 Put the chicken, glazed-side up, on the rack of the grill pan, and grill for 8 minutes until golden and sticky. Turn the chicken over, brush with the remaining glaze, then grill for another 6–8 minutes, or until the chicken is tender and cooked through. Serve straight away with wedges of lime, if you like.

• Per serving 242 kcalories, protein 12g, carbohydrate 66g, fat 9g, saturated fat 2g, fibre 1g, sugar 6g, salt 1.28g

Perfect for a weekday supper, there's virtually no cooking needed to produce this flavoursome, low-fat meal.

Peanut Chicken with Noodles

250g pack rice noodles
2 cooked chicken breasts, skinned and shredded
1 red pepper, seeded and sliced
2 handfuls of beansprouts
3 tbsp sweet chilli sauce
4 tbsp light soy sauce
4 spring onions, sliced
50g/2oz peanuts, roughly chopped, to serve
20g pack fresh coriander, leaves roughly chopped, to serve

Takes 15 minutes • Serves 4

1 Cook the noodles according to the packet instructions. Meanwhile, put the chicken and pepper in a microwave-proof dish and cover. Microwave on High for 2 minutes, or until piping hot.

2 Drain the noodles and tip into a bowl. Stir through the beansprouts. Whisk the chilli sauce and soy sauce together then stir through the noodles along with the chicken, pepper and spring onions. Scatter over the peanuts and coriander to serve.

• Per serving 407 kcalories, protein 27g, carbohydrate 59g, fat 9g, saturated fat 2g, fibre 2g, sugar 7g, salt 3.59g

If you want to use less bacon, stretch out four rashers with the back of a knife to make each one longer and thinner, then wrap just one around each chicken breast.

Mustard-stuffed Chicken

125g ball mozzarella, torn into small pieces
50g/2oz strong Cheddar, grated
1 tbsp wholegrain mustard
4 boneless skinless chicken breasts
8 rashers smoked streaky bacon

Takes 30 minutes • Serves 4 (easily halved)

1 Pre-heat the oven to 200°C/Gas 6/fan 180°C. Mix the cheeses and mustard together. Cut a slit in the side of each chicken breast then stuff with the mustard mixture.
2 Wrap each stuffed chicken breast with two bacon rashers – not too tightly, but firmly enough to hold the chicken together. Season, then place in a roasting tin, and roast for 20–25 minutes.

• Per serving 367 kcalories, protein 49g, carbohydrate none, fat 19g, saturated fat 10g, fibre none, added sugar none, salt 1.93g

Perfect for a lazy Sunday lunch, served with rocket or green beans, depending on the season, or your preference.

Maple Roast Chicken

750g/1lb 10oz small new potatoes, such as Charlottes, halved
2 small red onions, peeled and cut into wedges
1 head garlic, separated into cloves
2 tbsp olive oil
2 tbsp maple syrup
1 heaped tbsp wholegrain mustard
1 large red pepper, seeded and cut into chunky pieces
2 large courgettes, halved lengthways and very thickly sliced
few fresh thyme sprigs
4 large chicken legs, skin on

Takes 1¼ hours • Serves 4

1 Pre-heat the oven to 200°C/Gas 6/fan 180°C. Mix the potatoes and onions with all but two of the garlic cloves and half the oil in a large roasting tin then season to taste. Roast for 15 minutes.
2 Meanwhile, peel and crush the rest of the garlic and mix with the maple syrup, mustard and remaining oil and season to taste.
3 Toss the pepper, courgettes and the thyme with the potatoes, then arrange the chicken portions on top. Brush the chicken generously with the maple-syrup mixture. Roast for 45–60 minutes or until the chicken is golden and sticky and the vegetables are tender.

• Per serving 484 kcalories, protein 27g, carbohydrate 45g, fat 23g, saturated fat 6g, fibre 5g, sugar 13g, salt 1.83g

Slow-roasting is a great way to keep chicken moist, and adding potatoes to the roasting tin infuses them with lots of flavour.

Foolproof Slow-roast Chicken

butter, for greasing
1 chicken, about 1.6kg/3lb 8oz
1kg/2lb 4oz roasting potatoes,
peeled and halved or quartered,
if large
2 heads garlic, halved crossways
100ml/3½ fl oz white wine
100ml/3½ fl oz chicken stock
2 fresh rosemary sprigs
6 bay leaves
1 lemon, cut into wedges

Takes 2½ hours • Serves 4

1 Pre-heat the oven to 160°C/Gas 3/fan 140°C. Brush a large roasting tin with butter and smear a little over the skin of the chicken.
2 Place the chicken in the tin and arrange the potatoes around it. Put the halved garlic heads in the tin, pour over the white wine and stock, then cover with foil and place in the oven. Cook for 1 hour then remove the foil and give the potatoes a shake. Add the herbs and lemon wedges then cook uncovered for a further 50 minutes.
3 Turn the heat up to 220°C/Gas 7/fan 200°C. Cook for 30 minutes more, then remove the chicken and potatoes from the pan. Cover the chicken loosely with foil and leave to rest for at least 10 minutes before carving. Keep the potatoes warm. Serve with any pan juices poured over.

• Per serving 634 kcalories, protein 44g, carbohydrate 56g, fat 27g, saturated fat 9g, fibre 5g, sugar 4g, salt 1.76g

A super-quick, yet special dish that's perfect for weekday entertaining. Serve it with sauté potatoes and green beans.

Chicken with Herby Mascarpone

3 tbsp mascarpone cheese
1 tbsp finely chopped fresh rosemary
1 garlic clove, peeled and crushed
2 boneless chicken breasts, skin on
4 slices of prosciutto
splash of olive oil
juice of ½ lemon

Takes 25 minutes • Serves 2

1 Pre-heat the oven to 200°C/Gas 6/fan 180°C. Mix the mascarpone with the rosemary, garlic and seasoning. Lift the skin, without detaching. Put a spoonful of the cheese mix under the skin of each breast, then wrap with two slices of prosciutto.
2 Heat a non-stick frying pan, add the oil, and quickly brown the chicken on both sides. Transfer to a roasting tin, then finish in the oven for 15–20 minutes, or until the chicken is cooked through. Remove from the tin, cover with foil and leave to rest for 5 minutes.
3 Add the lemon juice to the roasting tin and stir over the heat, scraping up any crisp bits from the bottom. Spoon the juices over the chicken to serve.

• Per serving 339 kcalories, protein 37g, carbohydrate 3g, fat 20g, saturated fat 9g, fibre none, sugar 2g, salt 1.24g

The balsamic vinegar in this low-fat dish not only provides a rich gravy, but also helps tenderize the meat. Keep it healthy and serve with boiled rice and a green salad.

Balsamic Chicken with Orange

4 boneless skinless chicken breasts
2 tbsp olive oil
3 tbsp balsamic vinegar
150ml/¼ pint fresh orange juice
150ml/¼ pint hot chicken stock
2 tsp chopped fresh rosemary leaves
1 tbsp light muscovado sugar
knob of butter
orange segments and fresh rosemary sprigs, to garnish

Takes 25–35 minutes • Serves 4

1 Put the chicken between pieces of cling film and flatten slightly by pounding with the base of a pan. Unwrap and sprinkle on both sides with pepper. Heat the oil in a pan over a medium heat, then fry the chicken for 5 minutes, turning halfway.
2 Pour two tablespoons of the vinegar over the chicken, add the orange juice and stock and sprinkle with the rosemary and salt. Bring to the boil, lower the heat and bubble gently for 5 minutes, or until the chicken is cooked through, spooning the sauce over frequently and turning the chicken halfway.
3 Stir in the sugar, butter and remaining vinegar and sizzle for a few minutes until reduced and glossy. Put the chicken in a serving dish, spoon over the sauce and garnish with orange and rosemary to serve.

• Per serving 259 kcalories, protein 34g, carbohydrate 11g, fat 9g, saturated fat 3g, fibre trace, sugar 5g, salt 0.3g

Choose chicken breasts with plenty of unbroken skin to contain the stuffing or, if necessary, secure the filling with wooden cocktail sticks.

Spinach and Feta Chicken

4 boneless chicken breasts, skin on
85g/3oz frozen leaf spinach, defrosted
85g/3oz feta, crumbled
2 tbsp olive oil
2 tbsp pine nuts

Takes 30–35 minutes • Serves 4

1 Loosen the skin from the chicken. Drain the spinach in a sieve and press out as much water as possible. Mix with the feta and a little black pepper then stuff between the skin and flesh of the chicken, smoothing the skin back over the stuffing. Season the chicken all over with a little salt and pepper.

2 Heat the oil in a frying pan that has a lid. Add the chicken, skin-side down, and fry until the skin is browned. Turn it over and cook on the other side, then add the pine nuts and fry until lightly toasted. Add six tablespoons of water, then cover for 15–20 minutes, or until the chicken is cooked through.

• Per serving 308 kcalories, protein 36g, carbohydrate 2g, fat 18g, saturated fat 5g, fibre 1g, sugar 1g, salt 1.32g

A mouthwatering roast for a Sunday lunch with a Moroccan flavour.

Fragrant Roast Chicken

2 lemons, halved
2 heads garlic, halved crossways,
plus 2 garlic cloves, peeled and
crushed
1 chicken, about 1.8kg/4lb
50g/2oz butter, softened
2 tsp Ras-el-hanout spice mix
1 tsp smoked paprika (optional)
200g carton thick Greek yoghurt

Takes 1½ hours • Serves 6

1 Pre-heat the oven to 200°C/Gas 6/fan 180°C. Push half a lemon and half a garlic head into the cavity of the chicken, then put the chicken in a roasting tin. Mix the butter with the crushed garlic and half the spices and spread over chicken breast and legs. Season well. Put the remaining garlic around the chicken and roast for 1 hour.
2 Mix the remaining spices into the yoghurt and season. Remove the chicken from the oven and smother with the yoghurt. Spoon some of the juices over, add the remaining lemon to the tin. Roast for 15 minutes or until the yogurt is golden and set and the juices from the chicken run clear when the thickest part of a thigh is pierced with a skewer. Lift the chicken out, cover with foil, and leave to rest for 10 minutes before carving.

• Per serving 379 kcalories, protein 29g, carbohydrate 3g, fat 28g, saturated fat 12g, fibre none, sugar 2g, salt 1.96g

An utterly delicious combination of chicken, goats' cheese and bacon with tomatoes and courgettes tucked underneath for sweetness.

Goats' Cheese and Thyme-stuffed Chicken

2 boneless skinless chicken breasts
100g/4oz firm goats' cheese, such as Crottin de Chavignol
1 tsp fresh thyme leaves, plus 2–3 sprigs
4 thin-cut rashers streaky bacon
1–2 tbsp olive oil
2 courgettes, thinly sliced
250g/9oz vine tomatoes, thinly sliced
steamed Jersey Royals or any new potatoes, to serve

Takes 1 hour • Serves 2
(easily doubled)

1 Pre-heat the oven to 190°C/Gas 5/fan 170°C. Split each chicken breast almost in half along one long side, then open it out like a book. Bang them out with a rolling pin to flatten a little. Season on both sides. Put half the goats' cheese on one part of each piece of chicken and sprinkle with the thyme leaves. Fold the chicken over to enclose the cheese, then wrap each one in two rashers of bacon.
2 Lightly oil a roasting tin and arrange overlapping rows of courgettes and tomatoes over the bottom. Drizzle with olive oil and sprinkle with salt, pepper and thyme sprigs.
3 Sit the chicken on top of the vegetables and roast for 40–45 minutes, until the bacon is crisp and golden and the courgettes are tender. Serve with steamed potatoes.

• Per serving 476 kcalories, protein 52g, carbohydrate 6g, fat 27g, saturated fat 13g, fibre 2g, sugar 6g, salt 2.03g

Cooking the chicken upside-down at first keeps the breast succulent in this slow-cooked dish.

Chicken with Cider and Celery

small knob of butter
1 chicken, about 2kg/4lb 8oz
4 rashers smoked streaky bacon, chopped
1 onion, peeled and finely chopped
2 carrots, diced
fresh thyme sprig
2 celery hearts, quartered
150ml/¼ pint dry cider
300ml/½ pint chicken stock

Takes 2 hours • Serves 4

1 Pre-heat the oven to 190°C/Gas 5/fan 170°C. Heat the butter in a large flameproof casserole and brown the chicken slowly on all sides; this should take a good 10–15 minutes. Lift out the chicken, add the bacon and cook for 3–4 minutes until starting to crisp, then add the onion, carrots and thyme and continue to cook for 4–5 minutes until the vegetables soften.
2 Stir in the celery then nestle the chicken, breast-side down, among the vegetables. Pour over the cider and stock and bring to a simmer, then roast uncovered for 1 hour.
3 Turn the chicken the right way up and roast for 30 minutes more, or until the legs come away. Check the seasoning of the vegetables before serving with the chicken.

• Per serving 679 kcalories, protein 62g, carbohydrate 7g, fat 44g, saturated fat 14g, fibre 2g, sugar 6g, salt 1.37g

Wonderfully easy pies – the ultimate comfort food: crisp outside, succulent inside. Delicious.

Mini Chicken Pies

500g pack shortcrust pastry
2 boneless skinless cooked chicken breasts, shredded
85g/3oz peas, fresh or frozen
½ bunch asparagus, trimmed and cut into small bite-sized pieces
100g/4oz crème fraîche
1 egg, beaten

Takes 35–40 minutes, plus resting
Serves 8

1 Roll out the pastry until it is a little thinner than a £1 coin. Cut out eight 9cm/3½in discs and use to line eight holes of a muffin tin. Divide the chicken, peas and asparagus equally among the moulds, season and top each one with a spoonful of crème fraîche.
2 Cut out eight 7cm/2¾in discs to make lids for the pies. Lightly brush the edges of the pies with egg, cover with the lids and press down into the filling. Pinch the edges together to seal. Leave to rest in the fridge for 30 minutes, or up to 2 days if preparing in advance.
3 Pre-heat the oven to 200°C/Gas 6/fan 180°C. Brush the tops of the pies with more egg and bake for 30–35 minutes or until the pastry is crisp and golden. Serve warm or leave to cool.

• Per serving 396 kcalories, protein 15g, carbohydrate 30g, fat 25g, saturated fat 12g, fibre 2g, sugar 1g, salt 0.34g

Make a simple roast a stunning centrepiece for a supper party
and cook carrots under the chicken to give them a half-roasted,
half-braised sticky succulence.

Roast Chicken and Sticky Carrots

1 head garlic, separated into
cloves
2 bunches carrots, trimmed and
scrubbed
1 lemon, halved
1 tsp cumin seeds
1 tsp clear honey
85g/3oz butter, softened
bunch fresh parsley, leaves and
stalks separated
1 chicken, about 1.8kg/4lb
1 bay leaf

Takes 1¾ hours • Serves 4

1 Pre-heat the oven to 200°C/Gas 6/fan
180°C. Peel and chop two garlic cloves. Put
the carrots in a roasting tin, squeeze lemon
juice over, then toss in the garlic, cumin,
honey, half the butter and season.
2 Push parsley stalks into the cavity of the
chicken with the lemon halves, garlic and the
bay. Season the cavity. Sit the chicken on top
of the carrots and smear with the remaining
butter. Roast for 30 minutes, stir the carrots
and baste the breast with the juices. Roast
for 40–50 minutes or until the chicken is
cooked through. Remove, cover with foil, and
set aside for 10 minutes.
3 Chop the parsley leaves. Place with the
carrots in the tin over a low heat until sizzling.
Serve the chicken on top of the carrots.

• Per serving 588 kcalories, protein 42g, carbohydrate
3.6g, fat 45g, saturated fat 20g, fibre 0.1g, sugar 1g,
salt 0.79g

A truly indulgent dish that is perfect for preparing ahead as the flavour improves with freezing. Serve with mash.

Spanish Chicken

2 tbsp olive oil
8 chicken thighs, on the bone
1 red pepper, seeded and quartered
1 green pepper, seeded and quartered
2 garlic cloves, peeled and finely chopped
1 leek, trimmed and thickly sliced
225g/8oz cooked ham, cut into chunks
1 tsp paprika
300ml/½ pint red wine
400g can chopped tomatoes
1 tbsp tomato purée
2 fresh thyme sprigs or ½ tsp dried
2 tbsp chopped fresh parsley, to garnish

Takes 1½ hours • Serves 4

1 Pre-heat the oven to 160°C/Gas 3/fan 140°C. Heat the oil in a large flameproof casserole and fry the chicken over a high heat until browned all over. Remove with a slotted spoon and set aside. Reduce the heat slightly and add the peppers. Cook for 2–3 minutes, turning them, until they brown. Add the garlic and leek, cook for 2–3 minutes then stir in the ham.
2 Sprinkle over the paprika, cook for a couple of seconds, then add the wine and bubble for a few minutes. Tip in the tomatoes, purée and thyme and mix well. Add the chicken and just enough water to cover it and season. Bring to a simmer, cover and transfer to the oven. Cook for 1 hour or until the chicken is tender and cooked through. Serve garnished with the parsley.

• Per serving 896 kcalories, protein 71g, carbohydrate 9g, fat 59g, saturated fat 17g fibre 3g, added sugar none, salt 2.39g

A sophisticated and subtle dish that needs no accompaniment other than plain long grain rice and a simple green salad.

Lemon and Tarragon Chicken

300ml/½ pint dry white wine
1 onion, quartered
1 small bulb fennel, sliced, or 2 celery sticks, sliced
1 large carrot, cut into sticks
2 sprigs each fresh thyme, rosemary and tarragon
2 large bay leaves
about 100g/4oz smoked bacon pieces or rinds
½ tsp whole black peppercorns
1 tbsp bouillon powder or 2 stock cubes
1 chicken, about 2kg/4lb 8oz, excess fat removed

FOR THE SAUCE
2 egg yolks
142ml carton double cream
handful of tarragon leaves, chopped
1 tsp cornflour
juice of 1 lemon

Takes 1¾ hours • Serves 4

1 Put the wine, vegetables, herbs, bacon, peppercorns and bouillon in a pan. Bring to the boil and simmer for 10 minutes. Add the chicken and enough water to cover. Poach for 1¼ hours or until tender. Leave to stand off the heat for 15 minutes.

2 Lift out the chicken, strain the stock and measure 500ml/18fl oz into a clean pan. Reduce by half. Cut the bird into neat portions, discarding the skin, wing tips and backbone. Keep warm in a serving dish.

3 For the sauce, beat together the egg yolks, cream and tarragon. Mix in a quarter of the stock, then add this mixture back to the stock pan. Mix the cornflour with a little water, stir into the stock and simmer for 3–5 minutes until thickened. Off the heat, stir in the lemon juice, then pour over the chicken to serve.

• Per serving 689 kcalories, protein 62g, carbohydrate 3g, fat 42g, saturated fat 19g, fibre none, added sugar none, salt 1.35g

A cross between a roast and a stew: the chicken is fried until the skin is crisp, then the meat is simmered in wine and stock until juicy. Serve with potatoes roasted with grainy mustard.

Chicken Fricassee with Olives

4 chicken breasts, skin on
knob of butter
85g/3oz rashers smoked bacon, cut into small chunks
4 garlic cloves, peeled and roughly chopped
finely grated zest of 1 lemon
300ml/½ pint dry white wine
300ml/½ pint hot chicken stock
about 20 mixed olives
small handful of fresh tarragon leaves, to serve

Takes 50 minutes–1 hour • Serves 4

1 Season the chicken with plenty of ground black pepper, and salt if you want it. Heat the butter in a pan and brown the chicken over a medium heat. Remove the chicken from the pan, add the bacon and garlic and cook gently for about 2 minutes until just golden. Turn up the heat, add the lemon zest and wine, and simmer for a few minutes.
2 Reduce the heat and add the stock, olives and half the tarragon. Return the chicken to the pan and simmer gently for about 30 minutes or until the chicken is cooked through and the liquid has reduced. Serve hot, sprinkled with the remaining tarragon.

• Per serving 302 kcalories, protein 36g, carbohydrate 2g, fat 11g, saturated fat 4g, fibre 1g, added sugar none, salt 2.53g

Bursting with Mediterranean flavours, this is good served with rice or parsley-tossed tagliatelle.

Rosemary and Garlic Chicken

8 chicken thighs, skin on
1 tbsp plain flour, seasoned
2 tbsp olive oil
1 head garlic, separated into cloves
3 large fresh rosemary sprigs
300ml/½ pint dry white wine

Takes 50–60 minutes • Serves 4

1 Wipe the chicken with kitchen paper, trim away any excess skin with scissors, then toss in the seasoned flour.
2 Heat the oil in a large pan until searingly hot, add the chicken, skin-side down, and fry without moving the chicken until the skin is crisp and browned. Turn the chicken over and brown it on all sides (you may need to do this in batches). Add the peeled garlic and rosemary, then pour in the wine and season with salt and pepper. Bring to the boil, then reduce the heat and cover the pan. Simmer for 40–45 minutes or until the chicken is cooked through and the sauce has thickened.

• Per serving 744 kcalories, protein 57g, carbohydrate 5g, fat 50g, saturated fat 15g, fibre none, added sugar none, salt 0.89g

Just add new potatoes and a simple green salad of Little Gem lettuce and rocket lightly dressed with fresh lemon juice and olive oil as the perfect accompaniments.

Thyme Chicken with Mushrooms

4 part-boned chicken breasts, skin on
2 tbsp olive oil
10 fresh lemon thyme sprigs
plain flour, for lightly dusting
2 garlic cloves, peeled and chopped
400g/14oz chestnut mushrooms
142ml carton double cream

Takes 30–35 minutes • Serves 4

1 Rub the chicken with one tablespoon of the oil and season well. Strip the leaves from six thyme sprigs and sprinkle them evenly over the chicken. Dust with flour.
2 Heat the remaining oil in a frying pan, add the chicken skin-side down, and fry for 5 minutes. Continue cooking for 10–15 minutes, turning regularly, until the chicken is cooked through and the skin crisp and browned. Remove to a plate and keep warm.
3 Drain almost all of the oil from the pan. Add the garlic and mushrooms and toss over a high heat until starting to soften. Stir in the cream, add the remaining thyme, and season. Simmer for a few minutes until the mushrooms are cooked, then serve with the chicken.

• Per serving 347 kcalories, protein 35g, carbohydrate 3g, fat 21g, saturated fat 12g, fibre 2g, added sugar none, salt 0.62

Look for packets of tiny or baby new potatoes for these skewers, or pick out the smallest ones you can find. Get the best flavour for the 'no-cook' relish from vine-grown tomatoes.

Herbed Chicken Skewers

500g/1lb 2oz tiny new potatoes
3 tbsp each chopped fresh parsley, mint and chives
6 tbsp olive oil
2 tbsp fresh lemon juice
500g/1lb 2oz boneless skinless chicken breasts, cut into chunks
1 red onion, peeled
1 red pepper, seeded and cut into chunks
1 lemon, cut into 8 wedges

FOR THE RELISH
8 ripe tomatoes, seeded and finely chopped
2 green chillies, seeded and finely chopped
2 garlic cloves, peeled and chopped
4 tbsp olive oil
2 tbsp white wine vinegar

Takes 40–50 minutes • Serves 8

1 Cook the potatoes in boiling salted water for 10–12 minutes until just tender. Drain and leave to cool. Mix the herbs, oil, lemon juice, salt and pepper in a large bowl and add the chicken and potatoes. Mix well until everything is glistening. Cut the onion into six wedges then separate the layers on each wedge. Add the onion and pepper to the marinade and mix thoroughly.
2 To make the relish, mix the tomatoes, chillies, garlic, oil and vinegar with seasoning to taste.
3 Thread the chicken, potatoes, peppers and onion on to eight skewers, finishing each with a lemon wedge. Barbecue over a medium-high heat for 5–6 minutes on each side, or until the chicken is cooked through. Serve hot, with the tomato relish.

• Per serving 230 kcalories, protein 18g, carbohydrate 16g, fat 9g, saturated fat 2g, fibre 2g, added sugar none, salt 0.13g

The simple things in life are often the best, and that's exactly so with this recipe for the ultimate roast chicken.

Perfect Roast Chicken

2 unwaxed lemons, halved
1 organic or free-range chicken, about 1.8kg/4lb
6 bay leaves
small bunch fresh rosemary, broken into sprigs
2 whole heads garlic, halved crossways
1.5kg/3lb 5oz potatoes, peeled and quartered
2 tbsp sunflower or vegetable oil
50g/2oz butter, melted

Takes 1¾ hours • Serves 4

1 Pre-heat the oven to 190°C/Gas 5/fan 170°C. Prick one lemon half with a fork and push inside the chicken with half the herbs and one half-head of garlic.

2 Tip the potatoes and remaining garlic into a roasting tin, toss with the oil and season. Push the potatoes to the edges and sit the chicken in the middle. Brush butter all over the breasts and legs. Season.

3 Roast for 1 hour 10 minutes, brushing with more butter during cooking. The chicken is done when the juices run clear. Lift the bird from the tin and cover with foil.

4 Turn the oven up to 220°C/Gas 7/fan 200°C. Chop the remaining lemons and roast with the potatoes and remaining herbs for 15–20 minutes, until crisp.

• Per serving 800 kcalories, protein 50g, carbohydrate 67g, fat 39g, saturated fat 13g, fibre 5g, sugar 4g, salt 1.93g

This is a modern-day Kiev, shallow-fried rather than deep-fried to reduce the calories. Serve with a retro side dish – a Russian salad would be good.

Chicken Kiev

4 boneless skinless chicken breasts, mini fillets detached
100g/4oz plain flour
3 eggs, beaten
200g/8oz fine dry breadcrumbs
sunflower or vegetable oil, for shallow-frying
lemon wedges and watercress, to serve

FOR THE BUTTER STUFFING
50g/2oz butter, softened
1 garlic clove, peeled and crushed
small handful of fresh parsley, leaves finely chopped
2 fresh tarragon sprigs, leaves finely chopped
squeeze of fresh lemon juice

Takes 50–55 minutes, plus chilling
Serves 4

1 Beat all the ingredients for the butter, then divide into four and squash into flattish discs. Wrap in cling film; chill until hard.

2 Make an incision down the middle of each breast to make a pocket. Cover with cling film and flatten with a rolling pin.

3 Stuff each pocket with butter. Cover with a fillet and fold over the sides of the breast. Coat each breast in flour, egg, and breadcrumbs, then again in egg and breadcrumbs.

4 Pre-heat the oven to 200°C/Gas 6/fan 180°C. Shallow fry the Kievs in hot oil over a medium heat for 2–3 minutes on each side until dark golden. Drain on kitchen paper then bake in a roasting tin for 20 minutes or until firm when prodded at the widest part.

• Per serving 696 kcalories, protein 40g, carbohydrate 59g, fat 35g, saturated fat 11g, fibre 2g, sugar 2g, salt 1.47g

Ring the changes by adding crisp, bite-sized pieces of grilled bacon or sliced avocado for a creamier version. If using avocado, toss with a little fresh lemon juice and add to the salad just before dressing.

Chicken Caesar Salad

1 medium ciabatta loaf, torn into ragged croutons
3 tbsp olive oil
good pinch of sea salt
2 boneless skinless chicken breasts
1 large cos or romaine lettuce, leaves separated and torn into large pieces

FOR THE DRESSING
1 medium block Parmesan or Grana Padano, for grating and shaving (you won't use it all)
2 canned anchovies, mashed with a fork
1 garlic clove, peeled and crushed
5 tbsp mayonnaise
1 tbsp white wine vinegar

Takes 25 minutes • Serves 4

1 Pre-heat the oven to 200°C/Gas 6/fan 180°C. Toss the bread with two tablespoons of oil and the sea salt on a baking sheet. Bake for 8–10 minutes, turning often to ensure even browning.
2 Rub the chicken with the remaining oil and seasoning. Heat a griddle pan and cook the chicken for 8 minutes, turning once, until the juices run clear when the chicken is pierced.
3 Make the dressing. Grate a handful of cheese and mix with the rest of the dressing ingredients. Season to taste, and thin down with a few teaspoons of water if necessary.
4 Shave the cheese with a peeler. Put the lettuce in a large bowl with the chicken and croutons. Add the dressing and toss, then top with the shaved cheese.

• Per serving 590 kcalories, protein 37.3g, carbohydrate 28.6g, fat 37.1g, saturated fat 10.7g, fibre 2.4g, sugar 3.9g, salt 2.43g

This is a great for a summer barbecue, especially when teamed with succulent corn on the cob. Cut the cobs into large chunks, brush with oil and cook for 5–6 minutes until lightly charred, turning often.

Cajun Chicken

4 boneless skinless chicken breasts
1 tbsp paprika
¼ tsp cayenne pepper
1 tsp dried onion flakes
2 tsp dried thyme
1 tbsp sunflower oil
200g carton guacamole, to serve

Takes 20–25 minutes • Serves 4

1 Pat the chicken dry with kitchen paper, then cut criss-cross slashes in the smooth sides. Mix the spices with the onion and thyme and seasoning, then tip on to a plate. Brush the chicken on both sides with the oil, then coat all over with the spice mix.
2 Heat a barbecue, griddle pan or grill and cook the chicken for 5–6 minutes on each side or until cooked through. Serve each portion with a spoonful of guacamole.

• Per serving 190 kcalories, protein 34g, carbohydrate 2g, fat 5g, saturated fat 1g, fibre none, added sugar none, salt 0.22g

This is a quick and easy, low-fat version of the French classic.

Coq au Vin

4 boneless skinless chicken breasts
1 tbsp plain flour, seasoned
150ml/¼ pint chicken stock
1 tbsp mild olive or vegetable oil
250g pack chestnut mushrooms,
halved
few fresh thyme sprigs
150ml/¼ pint red wine

Takes 20 minutes • Serves 4

1 Toss the chicken in the flour, then tap off the excess. Mix one teaspoon of the excess flour with a little of the stock and set aside. Heat the oil in a deep frying pan and add the chicken, mushrooms and thyme. Cook over a medium-high heat for about 5 minutes until the chicken is golden, turning once.
2 Lift the chicken out, and set aside on a plate. Pour the wine and remaining stock into the pan, stir well and boil for 5 minutes until reduced by half. Add the flour and stock mix, and stir until the sauce thickens a little.
3 Put the chicken back in the pan, along with the juices from the plate. Simmer for 5 minutes or until the chicken is cooked through and the sauce is glossy.

• Per serving 216 kcalories, protein 35g, carbohydrate 5g, fat 5g, saturated fat 1g, fibre 1g, sugar 2g, salt 0.99g

Ths is a traditional, one-pot rice dish popular all over West Africa, but especially in Ghana. It is made with vegetables, chicken, fish or lamb, but always flavoured with the same ginger and chilli base.

Jollof Rice with Chicken

8 boneless skinless chicken thighs, cut into large pieces
3 tbsp vegetable or sunflower oil
1 large onion, peeled, halved and sliced
3 tbsp tomato purée
600ml/1 pint hot chicken stock
400g/14oz basmati rice, rinsed until the water runs clear
1 red pepper, seeded and thickly sliced
1 yellow pepper, seeded and thickly sliced
100g/4oz okra, topped, tailed and halved crossways
bunch fresh coriander, roughly chopped, to serve

FOR THE GINGER AND CHILLI BASE
2 garlic cloves, peeled and chopped
2 x 400g cans tomatoes
thumb-sized piece fresh root ginger, peeled and roughly chopped
1 Scotch bonnet chilli, halved and seeded
Takes 1¼ hours • Serves 4

1 Whiz the ingredients for the base in a food processor or blender until smooth. Season the chicken. Heat two tablespoons of the oil in a large, deep frying pan over a high heat, add the chicken and fry for 5 minutes until golden. Remove the chicken, add the remaining oil and fry the onion until soft, about 5 minutes.

2 Stir in the tomato purée and fry for 2 minutes, then stir in the puréed base and pour in the stock. Add the chicken, bring to the boil, and simmer for 15 minutes. Add the rice, cover with foil and a lid and simmer for 20 minutes.

3 Scatter the peppers and okra over the rice. Re-cover and cook for 10 minutes or until the rice is tender. Before serving, mix in the vegetables and sprinkle with the coriander.

• Per serving 705 kcalories, protein 51g, carbohydrate 98g, fat 15g, saturated fat 3g, fibre 5g, sugar 15g, salt 1.73g

A tasty stock is an essential part of this low-fat Chinese soup. Let it simmer with its flavourings for a really fragrant dish.

Chicken Noodle Soup

1.3 litres/2¼ pints chicken stock (home-made or fresh from the chiller cabinet)
2 star anise
3cm/1in piece fresh root ginger, sliced (no need to peel)
2 garlic cloves, bruised
2 bok choi (or 200g packet)
85g/3oz medium egg noodles
4 spring onions, finely sliced
100g/4oz cooked chicken, pulled into very thin shreds
splash of soy sauce
handful of fresh basil leaves
1 plump mild red chilli, seeded and finely sliced

Takes 30 minutes (not including the home-made stock) • Serves 4

1 Simmer the stock in a medium pan with the star anise, ginger and garlic for 10 minutes. Do not boil.
2 Meanwhile, trim the ends off the bok choi and separate the leaves, then roll the leaves up lengthways like a cigar, a few at a time. Shred very finely across with a sharp knife (both green and white parts), then steam over simmering water for 2 minutes.
3 While the bok choi steams, remove the flavourings from the stock with a slotted spoon and discard. Drop the noodles into the stock, stir to separate them then simmer for 4 minutes or until tender. Add the spring onions and chicken then season to taste with a splash of soy sauce. Ladle into bowls and scatter over the bok choi, basil and chilli.

• Per serving 132 kcalories, protein 19g, carbohydrate 5g, fat 4g, saturated fat 1g, fibre 1g, sugar 3g, salt 1.08g

Chopping chicken by hand can be time consuming, but it does create a much softer and juicier texture than blitzing it in a food processor.

Thai Minced Chicken Salad

2 stalks lemon grass
4 fresh kaffir lime leaves, stalks removed
2 red chillies, seeded
3 garlic cloves
fingertip-length piece fresh root ginger, peeled
4 boneless skinless chicken breasts
1 tbsp vegetable oil
1 tbsp sesame oil
1 tsp chilli powder
50ml/2fl oz fish sauce
1 red onion, peeled and chopped
3 tbsp fresh lime juice
handful each of fresh mint, basil and coriander leaves, roughly chopped

TO SERVE
3 Little Gem lettuces
1 cucumber, seeded and cut into strips lengthways
200g/8oz beansprouts
lime wedges

Takes 50 minutes • Serves 4

1 Roughly chop the lemon grass, lime leaves, chillies, garlic and ginger, then blitz them all in a food processor until everything is very finely chopped together. Chop the chicken into tiny pieces with a sharp knife.
2 Heat a wok over a high heat. Add the vegetable oil and the sesame oil, then the lemon-grass mixture, and fry briefly before adding the minced chicken and the chilli powder. Stir fry the chicken for 4 minutes, then splash in the fish sauce. Turn down the heat a little and allow the chicken and fish sauce to bubble together for another 4 minutes, stirring, then add the red onion and cook for another minute.
3 Remove from the heat, pour over the lime juice and toss in the herbs. Serve with the salad vegetables and lime wedges on the side.

• Per serving 261 kcalories, protein 39g, carbohydrate 9g, fat 8g, saturated fat 1g, fibre 2g, sugar 5g, salt 2.72g

If you have time, marinate the chicken beforehand. Toss the wings in the soy, sugar and vinegar the night before and leave in the fridge to soak up the flavours.

Sticky Chinese Wings

16 large chicken wings
125ml/4fl oz reduced-salt soy sauce
140g/5oz dark soft brown sugar
5 tbsp white wine vinegar
½ cucumber, peeled into
fine ribbons
cracked black pepper, to season
boiled or steamed rice, to serve

Takes 50 minutes • Serves 4

1 Pre-heat the oven to 220°C/Gas 7/fan 200°C. Toss the chicken wings in a roasting tin with the soy sauce, 125g/4oz of the sugar, two tablespoons of the vinegar and some cracked black pepper. Roast for 40 minutes, turning occasionally, until lacquered.
2 Meanwhile, bring the remaining sugar and vinegar to the boil for about 1 minute, until the sugar dissolves. Leave to cool, then toss with the cucumber ribbons. Serve the sticky wings with the cucumber and rice.

• Per serving 324 kcalories, protein 16g, carbohydrate 41g, fat 12g, saturated fat 3g, fibre none, sugar 40g, salt 3.57g

In Japan these chicken skewers are traditionally cooked over hot coals and basted constantly while cooking. They are served as a starter or as part of a main course.

Chicken Yakitori

8 thick spring onions, trimmed, white part cut into three pieces
3 boneless skinless chicken breasts, cut into strips

FOR THE GLAZE
75ml/3fl oz low-salt soy sauce
50ml/2fl oz mirin
50ml/2fl oz sake

8 bamboo/wooden skewers

Takes 35 minutes • Serves 4

1 Make the glaze. Bring all the ingredients to the boil in a pan and simmer for 3 minutes or until the glaze starts to become syrupy. Remove from the heat and leave to cool. Meanwhile, soak eight small bamboo or wooden skewers in warm water for about 30 minutes.

2 Heat the grill to high. Thread the skewers with alternating pieces of spring onion and chicken. Lay the skewers on a baking sheet and brush with a little glaze. Cook for about 12 minutes under the grill, turning every minute or so and brushing with glaze until the chicken is cooked through and looks sticky. Serve the skewers in a bowl and let everyone help themselves.

• Per serving 144 kcalories, protein 26g, carbohydrate 6g, fat 1g, saturated fat none, fibre none, sugar 2g, salt 2.43g

The ancho chillies used in Mexican cooking are made by drying vivid green poblano chillies. They are mild and slightly sweet and well worth looking out for.

Chicken Enchiladas

4 boneless skinless chicken breasts
4 ancho chillies, halved and seeded
2 plum tomatoes, halved
1 onion, peeled and chopped
2 garlic cloves, peeled
3 tbsp blanched almonds, plus extra for serving
2 tbsp vegetable oil
2 tsp raisins
1 tsp dried oregano
1 tsp ground cumin
½ tsp ground cinnamon
small piece dark chocolate
375g pack fresh tortillas
fresh coriander sprigs and lime wedges, to serve

Takes 50 minutes • Serves 4

1 Poach the chicken in 300ml/½ pint water, for 20 minutes, turning once. Remove, saving the liquid, and shred with a fork.
2 Soften the chillies in boiling water for 20 minutes. Drain and chop, then put in a blender with 100ml/4fl oz poaching liquid. Dry fry the tomatoes in a deep frying pan for 5 minutes until blistered. Add to the blender. In the same frying pan, cook the onion, garlic and almonds in the oil for 5 minutes. Stir in the raisins, oregano and spices, cook for 2 minutes, then add to the blender and whiz.
3 Pour the mixture back into the pan, stir in the chocolate and 350ml/12fl oz poaching liquid and simmer for 20 minutes. Warm the tortillas, pile the chicken on top, then spoon over the sauce and roll up.

• Per serving 569 kcalories, protein 29g, carbohydrate 69g, fat 21g, saturated fat 6g, fibre 4g, sugar 4g, salt 3.27g

Vegetables can be added with the coconut milk in this authentic curry. Try green beans, thinly sliced small potatoes, aubergine or frozen peas.

Thai Chicken Curry

1 tbsp vegetable oil
2 shallots or 1 small onion, peeled and thinly sliced
3–4 tsp Thai red curry paste
4 boneless skinless chicken breasts, cut into bite-sized pieces
1 tbsp fish sauce
1 tsp sugar (whatever you have, although brown is best)
1 stalk lemon grass, very thinly sliced
4 kaffir lime leaves (fresh or freeze-dried)
400ml can coconut milk
20g pack fresh coriander, leaves roughly chopped
Thai jasmine rice, to serve

Takes 30–40 minutes • Serves 4

1 Heat the oil in a wok and fry the shallots or onion for 3–5 minutes until soft. Stir in three teaspoons of curry paste and cook for 1 minute, stirring all the time. Add the chicken and stir until coated. Add the fish sauce, sugar, lemon grass, lime leaves and coconut milk and bring slowly to the boil.
2 Reduce the heat and simmer, uncovered, for 15 minutes or until the chicken is cooked through. Stir the curry a few times while it cooks, to stop it sticking and to keep the chicken submerged.
3 Taste the curry and add a little more curry paste and salt if you think it needs it. Stir half the coriander leaves into the curry and sprinkle the rest over the top. Serve with Thai jasmine rice.

• Per serving 372 kcalories, protein 36.2g, carbohydrate 5.6g, fat 23g, saturated fat 15.1g, fibre 0.1g, sugar 4.5g, salt 1.67g

A classic Jamaican dish, usually served with rice and peas.
Cook long grain rice in coconut milk and water, then toss with red
kidney beans, chopped spring onions, chilli flakes and thyme.

Jamaican Jerk Chicken

4 boneless skinless chicken breasts
juice of 1 lime
fresh coriander sprigs and lime
wedges, to garnish

FOR THE MARINADE
4 spring onions, chopped
2 red chillies, seeded and
chopped
1 tbsp ground allspice
2 tsp ground cinnamon
½ tsp dried thyme
2 tsp light muscovado sugar
1 tbsp sunflower oil

Takes 45 minutes, plus marinating
Serves 4 (easily doubled)

1 Make the marinade. Blitz all the ingredients in a food processor or blender until fairly smooth. Add a little salt if you like. You could use a pestle and mortar, but it's harder work.
2 Spread the marinade evenly over the chicken in a shallow dish. Cover and then marinate in the fridge for at least 30 minutes, preferably overnight.
3 Heat a griddle pan or barbecue, remove the chicken from the fridge and pour over the lime juice. Cook the chicken slowly for 25–30 minutes, turning once. Serve hot or cold with coriander sprigs and lime wedges.

• Per serving 207 kcalories, protein 34g, carbohydrate 7g, fat 5g, saturated fat 1g, fibre 0.1g, sugar 2.5g, salt 0.2g

This comforting Jewish soup from Poland is traditionally made for a special meal called Seder, which is held at the beginning of Passover.

Chicken Dumpling Soup

4 chicken thighs, skin on, bone in
1 carrot
1 onion
handful of fresh dill, to serve

FOR THE MATZO BALLS
50g/2oz matzo meal, plus extra for shaping
½ tsp salt
2 eggs, beaten
2 tbsp vegetable oil
2 tbsp sparkling water

Takes 2½ hours • Serves 4

1 Put the chicken, carrot and onion in a pan, cover with 1.5 litres/2¾ pints water and bring to the boil. Skim, then simmer for 40 minutes, skimming often. Remove the chicken and shred the meat with a fork. Return the bones to the pan and simmer for 1½ hours. Strain and add seasoning.

2 Mix the matzo meal and salt in a bowl. Mix the eggs, oil and water together and stir into the matzo meal. Cover with cling film and chill for 30 minutes, or until a soft dough forms.

3 Dust your hands with matzo meal then loosely shape the matzo dumpling into 12 balls. Drop them one at a time into a large pan of boiling salted water, cover and simmer for 30 minutes. Transfer the balls to the soup with a slotted spoon, add the chicken and heat through. Sprinkle with dill before serving.

• Per serving 200 kcalories, protein 14g, carbohydrate 15g, fat 10g, saturated fat 2g, fibre 1g, added sugar none, salt 0.8g

Don't worry about the rice sticking on the bottom of the pan – this is how it is meant to be.

Persian Chicken Pulao

400g/14oz best-quality basmati rice
85g/3oz butter
2 onions, peeled and thinly sliced
3 tbsp vegetable oil
½ tsp turmeric
200g/8oz large split lentils, preferably yellow channa
850ml/1½ pints hot chicken stock
140g/5oz sultanas
6 boneless skinless chicken thighs, cut into large pieces

Takes 1 hour 10 minutes • Serves 6

1 Cover the rice with cold, salted water. Bring to the boil and add half the butter. Simmer for 5 minutes, then drain and rinse.
2 Soften the onions in two tablespoons of the oil in a large pan. Add the turmeric and lentils, fry for 1 minute, then stir in the stock. Cover and simmer for 20 minutes or until the lentils have softened. Tip in the sultanas and chicken, cover and cook for 10 minutes.
3 Return the empty rice pan to a medium heat and add the remaining butter and oil. When the butter foams, put half the rice back in the pan and pat down. Spread the chicken and lentils on top, then the remaining rice. Pour over any liquid from the chicken, cover the pan tightly and cook gently for 30 minutes or until the rice at the bottom is *tardigh* – crisp and dark golden. Stir before serving.

• Per serving 667 kcalories, protein 34g, carbohydrate 92g, fat 21g, saturated fat 9.1g, fibre 4g, added sugar none, salt 0.94g

In this authentic Indian dish the chicken is cooked without its skin which is good news for the waistline.

Chilli Chicken Curry

1 onion, peeled and roughly chopped
knob of fresh root ginger, peeled and roughly chopped
2 garlic cloves, peeled and chopped
1 tsp cumin seeds
2 tbsp vegetable oil
½ tsp turmeric
½ tsp hot chilli powder or ¼ tsp cayenne pepper
227g can chopped tomatoes
350g/12oz potatoes, peeled and cut into rough chunks
500g/1lb 2oz boneless skinless chicken breasts, cut into bite-sized chunks
½ tsp garam masala
2 tbsp chopped fresh coriander
basmati rice boiled with 2 cinnamon sticks, to serve

Takes 50 minutes–1 hour • Serves 4

1 Blitz the onion, ginger and garlic in a food processor with one tablespoon of water until smooth. Fry the cumin seeds in oil for a few seconds. Stir in the onion purée and brown over a medium heat, adding a splash of water if it starts to catch.

2 Sprinkle in the turmeric and chilli, add the tomatoes and fry for 5 minutes. Stir in the potatoes and 250ml/9fl oz hot water, then cover and cook for 10 minutes.

3 Add the chicken and garam masala, and simmer for 15–20 minutes or until the chicken is cooked through. Season with salt. Tip into a bowl, scatter over coriander and serve with the basmati rice.

• Per serving 283 kcalories, protein 34g, carbohydrate 21g, fat 8g, saturated fat 1g, fibre 2g, added sugar none, salt 0.35g

This chicken is seasoned with chermoula, an authentic Moroccan spice mix. You should be able to find it at most large supermarkets.

Moroccan Chicken

1 unwaxed lemon, halved
2 tbsp olive oil
1 garlic clove, peeled and crushed
small knob of fresh root ginger, peeled and finely chopped
2 tsp chermoula spice mix
2 chicken legs
1 onion, peeled and sliced
225ml/8fl oz hot chicken or vegetable stock
1 tsp clear honey
handful of green olives, pitted
couscous and chopped fresh coriander leaves, to serve

Takes 50 minutes • Serves 2 (easily doubled)

1 Finely chop one lemon half, including the skin. Work to a paste with one tablespoon of the oil, the garlic, ginger and chermoula using a mortar and pestle or a small blender.
2 Heat the remaining oil in a large frying pan over a medium heat. Season the chicken and cook, skin-side down, for 5 minutes until golden. Turn the chicken over, add the onion, and cook for 5 minutes until the onion is soft.
3 Add the paste to the pan and cook for 1 minute until fragrant. Add the stock and honey then bring to the boil. Lower the heat, cover and cook for 20–30 minutes, or until the chicken is tender and the sauce is thick and glossy (uncover the pan for the final 5 minutes). Stir in the olives and the juice of the remaining lemon half. Serve hot, with couscous and a sprinkling of coriander.

• Per serving 476 kcalories, protein 31g, carbohydrate 11g, fat 35g, saturated fat 8g, fibre 2g, sugar 78g, salt 1.74g

These chunky chicken quesadillas make a substantial snack or casual lunch, or even a delicious dinner for all the family when accompanied by a spicy bean salad.

Chicken Quesadillas

1 tsp olive oil
1 shallot, peeled and sliced
100g/4oz chorizo sausage, diced
2 cooked chicken breasts, skinned and shredded
2 plum tomatoes, diced
320g pack soft tortillas
200g/8oz Cheddar, grated
small bunch fresh coriander, leaves roughly chopped

Takes 25 minutes • Serves 6

1 Heat the oil in a pan and cook the shallot and chorizo for 5 minutes until the shallot is softened. Stir in the chicken and tomatoes. Remove from the heat.

2 Put half the tortillas on to baking sheets. Spread a little chicken mixture on each one and scatter over the cheese and coriander. Sandwich with the remaining tortillas.

3 Pre-heat the oven to 180°C/Gas 4/fan 160°C. Cook the tortillas for 3 minutes. Using a fish slice, turn each one over. Cook for 3 minutes more until both sides are golden. Serve warm, sliced into wedges.

• Per serving 424 kcalories, protein 29g, carbohydrate 30g, fat 22g, saturated fat 10g, fibre 2g, sugar 1g, salt 2.42g

Index

214   Index